A FIST IN THE
HORNET'S NEST

A FIST IN THE HORNET'S NEST

On the Ground in Baghdad Before, During and After the War

RICHARD ENGEL

NEW YORK

Library of Congress Cataloging-in-Publication Data

ISBN: 1-4013-0115-0

Hyperion books are available for special promotions and premiums. For details contact Hyperion Special Markets, 77 West 66th Street, 11th floor, New York, New York, 10023, or call 212-456-0133.

FIRST EDITION

10 9 8 7 6 5 4 3 2 1

For my parents, Nina and Peter

ACKNOWLEDGMENTS

GRATEFUL THANKS TO JULIANNE GALICH, and to the editors, reporters, producers, cameramen and executives of NBC News, ABC News and The World (WGBH-Boston/BBC); Richard Leibner at N. S. Bienstock; and the people at Hyperion. Thanks, too, to David Halberstam for providing the book's title.

A FIST IN THE
HORNET'S NEST

INTRODUCTION

THE TANK SHELL THAT SMASHED into the Palestine Hotel sent bits of concrete pouring down onto the roof of a tent, where I'd been sitting, urgently discussing with my friend Ismail how we could stay safe on this, the heaviest day of the fighting we'd seen in Baghdad.

"We've been hit," I thought when I heard the explosion above me. It was so loud that I instinctively bent over and covered my head with my hands. I had no idea who had fired on us, or with what. More important, I didn't know if there was more of it on the way.

I ran out of the tent onto the grassy lawn in the shadow of the Palestine, craning my neck to see what had slammed into the upper floors of the hotel. I struggled to snap on my black helmet as I ran to record what was going on around me with my handheld digital video (DV) camera. The video was very shaky. I was breathing hard.

When I first saw the destruction, I was sure it had been caused by a relatively small weapon, perhaps a rocket-propelled grenade. The explosive had hit the tower of the hotel where the guest rooms were located. The Palestine consisted of a large rectangular base, which housed the lobby, the restaurant, a coffee shop, several conference rooms and a boutique that sold Iraqi souvenirs, including Bedouin clothing, checkered headscarves and stuffed camels. The eighteen-story tower grew out of the middle of the base. The tank shell had shorn off the corner of the tower's fourteenth and fifteenth floors. The damage also appeared to have been made by something fired from the ground and not by the many fighter jets and helicopters that had been ferociously attacking Baghdad all morning. I noted these observations in my head as I ran around the hotel holding my little DV camera—my flak jacket thumping against me with each stride and my helmet slipping off my head—trying to figure out if the time had finally come to flee the hotel for one of the safe houses I had established.

From where I stood staring up at the building, I could hear a female journalist screaming in panic. She was one floor above me, standing on the roof over the hotel's lobby and conference rooms. It was effectively a balcony where most of the broadcast journalists did our transmissions. She was yelling, "We're all going to die! We're all going to die!" She'd snapped.

The strike on the Palestine was the critical moment of what had already been a harrowing day.

I'd woken that morning to the sound of US fighter jets tearing through the sky over the hotel. It sounded like a giant zipper. The jets were buzzing so low that the glass balcony door in my room trembled like the top of a snare drum. I rolled out of my bed, belly to the floor, and inched over to the balcony, where I watched the jets swoop over Baghdad like birds of prey, releasing bombs from their talons. I saw those bombs crumple the buildings they hit, turning the concrete and glass structures into what looked like heaps of freshly tilled topsoil out of which sprouted mushroom clouds of pure white smoke.

A journalist had already been killed that day in Baghdad. American forces had destroyed the office of the Arab television network al-Jazeera in the early-morning hours, killing a reporter. Al-Jazeera's office—along with the bureau of the rival Arabic-language satellite television network Abu Dhabi—was across the Tigris River from the Palestine in a much more dangerous part of the city. Thus far, Baghdad's western bank had been attacked by US forces every day of the war. It was clearly the best place in the city to take pictures—some of the images the two Arab networks broadcast were nothing less than extraordinary—but the location was far too risky. They were killing themselves to compete with each other. I'd offered the Abu Dhabi team a chance to stay with me at the Palestine. I told them that I thought the two networks had been pushing their luck too far throughout the war. "You're too close," I said.

This is not to justify what happened. I've been told that both al-Jazeera and Abu Dhabi had given the Pentagon the global positioning system (GPS) coordinates of their bureaus in Baghdad. The Americans, therefore, should have known where they were. The US military's attitude, however, was that anyone who wasn't embedded with them was in Iraq at his or her own risk.

That day—April 8, 2003—I also witnessed what was for me the most terrifying air attack carried out by what I suspect may be the most frightening plane in the US arsenal: the A-10 Thunderbolt II, more commonly called the A-10 Warthog because of its stubby, inelegant shape and the grunting noise it makes when it fires its anti-tank machine gun. From my balcony I'd watched the stocky little plane fly low and slow over the city, dropping rows of flares to divert heat-seeking anti-aircraft rockets fired at it; none were. The pilot also performed acrobatics to protect the plane, swooping up and down and from side to side as if in an air show. The A-10 Warthog is armed with a Gatling gun in its nose that fires huge 30mm bullets hardened with depleted uranium that penetrate tank armor. The spinning gun fires bullets so quickly that it's impossible to distinguish the sound of the individual shots, and the rapid firing blends together to make a low-pitch grinding sound like an upstairs neighbor dragging a heavy sofa across the floor. I watched the plane unleash its Gatling gun on the Iraqi ministry of planning, which like all ministries at this stage in the war was empty. The barrage of bullets made it look as if someone were cutting the ministry in half with a giant chain saw. I wondered at the time why a plane designed to destroy tanks was firing on an empty building. I cynically suspected the pilot of testing out the Warthog's capabilities, "letting her rip," so to speak.

The Warthog wasn't the only American hunter prowling the sky and providing close air support to the advancing troops that day. I also watched a pair of US attack helicopters in action a few miles to the south of the Palestine. I'd filmed them circling each other like bees over a flower, their noses pointing down toward the streets. They were occasionally firing into the city, destroying anyone and anything that threatened the tanks and armored personnel carriers (APCs) filled with marines advancing below them.

Throughout the day, I'd heard gunfire crackling around the hotel and Iraqi artillery being launched from behind a row of nearby buildings. The artillery shells had been whizzing overhead on their way to the western bank, where the US Army had taken up position one day earlier. I suspected many of the artillery shells were probably landing on Iraqi homes in the area.

Earlier, I'd still had the feeling that the Palestine was in the calm eye of the hurricane, albeit an eye that was shrinking by the minute. That changed when the hotel itself was shelled.

I rushed back to the tent to see what Ismail thought about

the attack on the Palestine. Ismail—a stocky Turk in his forties with a crew cut, a thick neck and round sensitive eyes—was in charge of the Turkish satellite uplink service I'd been using for my live shots, a company called IHA. The tent we were in was IHA's makeshift office, equipped with a television set, a satellite telephone, a bed, a small refrigerator and an area with a carpet for Ismail and his team of five cameramen and satellite-uplink engineers to pray; they were all Muslims. All of his equipment was powered by several generators that Ismail had rigged with auxiliary gas tanks so they could run twenty-four hours a day. Ismail had once been an officer in the Turkish military and still acted the part. He was firm, always spoke his mind and thought of his team before himself. His crew ate together and relied on Ismail to settle all disputes. If the team had only three pieces of bread, they were given to Ismail to divide equally.

I told Ismail that I suspected Iraqi *fedayeen,* officially known as *Fedayeen Saddam* or the Saddam Commandos, had fired a shoulder-launched rocket at the hotel from one of the nearby buildings, but I wasn't satisfied with this explanation. I couldn't understand why they'd bother to shoot at a hotel full mostly of Western reporters. We weren't a threat to them. "Could it be an eye for an eye for killing the al-Jazeera reporter?" I wondered.

Ismail had another, more ominous theory. He suspected that the director general of the Iraqi Information Ministry and press center, Uday al-Ta'e, was responsible for the attack. Ismail had seen Uday lingering below the part of the hotel that had been hit a few minutes before the attack. Uday had been searching for a camera that had been providing pictures to the Fox cable news network. Uday had kicked Fox out of Iraq before the start of the war, apparently for being too supportive of US military action, and had specifically ordered journalists not to film from their hotel rooms. But Fox had managed to continue broadcasting live pictures from Baghdad, even though the network didn't have a correspondent in the city. There had been a camera on the balcony of one of the rooms that had been hit. Ismail believed that if Uday suspected the camera on the balcony belonged to Fox, he was capable of ordering the attack to shut it down and send a message to other journalists to follow his dictates or else. It was a chilling thought. Even though I'd always had an amiable relationship with Uday and he didn't seem to be a sinister combination of evil and lazy, like some other Iraqi government officials, Ismail's theory did seem plausible. Since the start of the war, I'd been haunted by thoughts of what Iraqi officials might do to Western reporters during the final stages of the war when it became clear that the Saddam regime was fighting for its life. Now that we had clearly arrived at that critical stage, I was especially concerned, as one of less than a dozen American reporters still in Baghdad. I'd also noticed Uday looking despondent over the last twenty-four hours, sitting alone at night in his office in the lobby of the Palestine. I feared that Uday had realized that soon he would be an outlaw. I worried Uday might have become a desperate man.

Shouts from the hotel lobby interrupted my discussion with Ismail. Journalists were bringing down our colleagues who'd been injured by the shelling. I saw a cameraman rushed out of the hotel and loaded into a waiting car. He was wrapped in a bloody bedsheet. His eyes were expressionless and his face was blank. Other reporters came out, several splattered with blood. It was hard to tell who was injured and who was offering relief. This was the image I had in my mind when I walked in front of the live camera to do a report for *Good Morning America*. The editors told me in my earpiece that General Buford Blount of the Army's Third Infantry Division had announced that one of his tanks had fired the shell at the Palestine Hotel in response to shots coming from there.

"But that's not true," I said.

"That's what the general is saying," I was told. "He said the tank crew responded to sniper and RPG [rocket-propelled grenade] fire from the hotel.

"After the tank fired," they told me the general said, "the shooting stopped."

I hadn't heard a single shot come from the hotel. None of the journalists had. That's what I said on air.

After the broadcast I climbed the stairs to the fourteenth floor to see the damage. The power had been out for several days and emergency generators were operating the elevators, but I didn't want to risk getting stuck. I walked into the damaged room and onto the balcony, where I saw my colleagues' blood amid the shattered glass and broken concrete. From the balcony I could also see the tank that had fired at us.

That night we held a candlelight vigil on the lawn for our colleagues who died of their wounds. Many of the journalists were crying. An Iraqi man stood up to make a speech during the vigil. Everyone fell silent. He started shouting, banging his fists on the table we'd set up for the candles and calling us mercenaries who were only interested in making money off the blood of the Iraqi people. I went upstairs to my room bitter at the world and wrote in my journal:

April 8:

I watched US tanks and APCs rolling on the other side of the river today. They were moving back and forth, kicking up dust and smoke. Then I saw two tanks take up positions on the bridge.

Then I heard about the al-Jazeera reporter. I'd just spoken yesterday to the Abu Dhabi correspondent, telling him that I thought his office was no longer safe. He said, "but al-Jazeera is there."

That poor reporter, he'd just gotten here a few days ago.

Then the hotel itself was hit. I was down in the IHA tent. I ran outside. There didn't seem to be too much damage. I thought it was probably an RPG fired by the Iraqis. Ismail suspected foul play from Uday.

I went up to the room on the 14th floor. The glass

balcony door was shattered. The balcony itself was crumbling. There was a pool of blood and blood on the shards of glass. There were long sweeping tracks of bloodstains on the carpet where the injured reporter had evidently been dragged. It was the blood of a Spanish guy from Telecinco. His blood was also on the sheets that the others had used to help him. His leg had nearly been blown off. His bone was broken, his leg hanging on by a piece of flesh. The Reuters guy in the room on the 15ᵗʰ floor was wounded in the belly. His guts were hanging out. He died after that.

US General Blount said there was sniper and RPG fire coming from the hotel. This is nothing less than total bullshit. There was no fire and I've been here all day. Then a general at the [US Central Command] briefing in Doha said there had been "hostile intent" from the hotel and that the army does not "target" journalists. If it was not "targeted" then why was the army taking "wild shots" at a hotel full of journalists? The tank commander probably thought the camera was a Stinger missile or some type of shoulder-launched rocket. The stinger has a lens similar to a TV Betacam. But didn't he know this hotel is full of reporters with TV cameras?

War, life and death are too important to be put in the hands of some 19-year-old who has never left the States. It's too important to be left to children. The soldier who fired the shell probably isn't old enough to have a beer in a bar, but he can fire a tank!

I put down my pen and tried to catch a few hours of sleep. I thought about the reporters who had died. They were not my friends, though I'd seen them around. But I did know that I could just as easily have been one of the casualties. I wondered how I'd come to be in Iraq and how we as a country had arrived here too.

CHAPTER ONE

THE JOURNEY THAT BROUGHT me to Iraq started in
Egypt. I moved to Cairo after graduating from college in
1996 with a Bachelor of Arts in international relations and no
real clue what I was getting into. I didn't speak a word of Arabic
or have any contacts in the Middle East. I'd set off with a thousand dollars in cash wallpapering my pockets and tucked into a
money belt around my waist, and landed at Cairo International
Airport armed with two suitcases of clothing destined to be
ruined by Cairo's all-penetrating filth, a worn copy of Nikos
Kazantzakis's inspiring book *Zorba The Greek* and a hope that
I'd be able to make myself into a foreign correspondent. I've long
believed that opportunities must be made and that if proverbial
"doors" don't open, it's best to kick them down. That's been my
philosophy since I was a young boy struggling with dyslexia,

which often left me frustrated and demoralized. Well-intentioned but somewhat patronizing teachers and school administrators had told my parents at the time that private school would have been too difficult for me and that I would never learn a foreign language. It annoyed me so much I had to prove them wrong.

I had no real experience in journalism before arriving in Cairo. I'd spent one summer as an unpaid intern at CNN Business News (now CNNfn) in New York City, and banged out a handful of insignificant articles for *The Stanford Daily*. These brief forays into journalism had nonetheless been enough to whet my appetite for the field. The prospect of learning about new subjects and having the privilege of riding the train of history rather than watching it pass me had tremendous appeal. I didn't want to break into journalism in the traditional way. At twenty-two, I was impatient and restless. So I vagabonded off to Cairo. The logic was the same as starting my career in a small market: There would be fewer journalists competing for stories. I figured if my Arab escapade didn't work out, I could always return home and try to find employment as a business consultant. It was 1996 after all. There were plenty of jobs.

My choice of the Middle East was strategic. I guessed that the Middle East would be a hot story in the post–Cold War world. I'd also considered setting up shop in China, but my impression at the time was that many of the stories Americans were interested in from Asia were economic and financial. I didn't want to be a business reporter, which I would unscientifically classify as no fun at all. As the years passed in Cairo, however, what I had initially assumed would be a way to make a break developed into a fascination with the Middle East and the cultures, splendors and horrors that make the region such a pivotal part of our world.

After taking a few Arabic lessons in Cairo without making the progress I'd hoped for, I moved into a poor neighborhood, ironically named *Sahafiyeen*, which means in Arabic the "journalists' district." I rented an apartment on the seventh floor of a plain, prison-like cement building that looked like it might have been designed by a graduate of the Stalin school of architecture. It had no elevator; almost no water pressure (often no water at all); foul-smelling, 1960s-vintage furniture (if I slapped a cushion, clouds of dust filled the air); and a live-in colony of fearless, scarab-sized cockroaches. I once saw one so huge I could actually hear it walking across the hardwood floors. The giant bug shuffled slowly and looked at me haughtily when I confronted it armed with a slipper. Air-conditioning was an impossible dream. The lobby of the building was often splattered with sheep or goat's blood courtesy of a nearby butcher who killed the animals for customers on demand. Every year during the Eid al-Adha, or feast of the sacrifice, when Muslims traditionally sacrifice an animal to commemorate the Biblical and Koranic accounts of God commanding Abraham to slaughter his son Isaac, it looked like there'd been a multiple homicide in my building.

Within a week in Sahafiyeen I became—no exaggeration— the most popular person in the neighborhood. My apartment was always vibrating with activity. Locals came in droves to drink tea, smoke cheap Cleopatra cigarettes (I supplied both gratis), stomp out hordes of my live-in cockroaches and check out the new young American who'd landed in their neighborhood like a Martian. Many people asked me to help them obtain visas to the United States, assuming I had diplomatic privileges and a direct line to the president. One time I jokingly told a new acquaintance that I'd call President Clinton and see what I could arrange for him. The man looked excited and asked me several times if I'd followed up on it. Sarcasm is little understood in the Arab world. Other people in the neighborhood offered their services as guides, dragomen, electricians, plumbers, teachers and handymen of all sorts. I learned after receiving a few offended glances that my untrained tutors liked to be called professors, and that anyone who knew which end of a screwdriver to hold liked to be called an engineer. Surrounded by so many "engineers," it was a wonder I lived in such a dump. The majority of the people in the neighborhood—who would drop by my apartment unannounced and stay for hours smoking cigarettes and drinking tea loaded with sugar—were both curious and somewhat flattered that an American had chosen to live among them instead of the wealthier Cairenes, whom they deeply resented. Egypt's nouveau riche not only stood out in stark contrast from the impoverished majority of the population, but they often made the disparity far more noticeable with their garish tastes for Mercedes with tinted windows, gold-leaf–encrusted reproductions of Louis XIV love seats and throne-like chairs (dubbed the Louie Farouq style by local expatriates) and condescending behavior.

I felt accepted in my new neighborhood, although I had some trouble getting accustomed to the squalor. My street was paved, but many of the narrow alleys in the warren-like area were merely packed dirt that would turn to sticky mud during the midwinter rains. The municipality never picked up the trash, forcing locals to set it on fire, giving the neighborhood a unique acrid smell that clung to the insides of the nostrils. I also had to accept the fact that I no longer had any personal space or privacy. My army of "engineers" talked to me at breath-smelling range and held my hand when we spoke or walked in the streets, which were littered with empty silver-lined bags of potato chips, rotten vegetables and thousands of cigarette butts and patrolled by two-foot-tall stray dogs with bent ears. My friends, advisors, bodyguards, tutors (everyone carved out a role) also demanded to know everything about my life and movements. If I went to a coffee shop that I didn't normally go to, everyone wanted to know why and if I'd do it again. I felt very looked after.

Unlike poor districts in the United States, which tend to be centers of crime and drugs, underprivileged areas in the Arab world are known as *Shaabi* neighborhoods, or "of the people." The name describes them perfectly. The English translation would be "popular" neighborhoods, although I've never found American slums to be especially popular. *Shaabi* areas in Egypt, on the other hand, generally have fewer social problems than the wealthy neighborhoods. Society in places like Saha-fiyeen was tightly knit, devoutly Islamic and thoroughly safe. I firmly believe that if I'd been robbed, assaulted or harassed in any way, the locals would have hunted down those responsible and beaten them severely. I once saw a mob pummel a man of about thirty a few blocks from my building. The man had tied a wire coat hanger to a string, which he'd been swinging up to people's balconies to yank down their *galabeyas* (the flowing pajama-like suits commonly worn mainly in rural and poor parts of Egypt) from clotheslines as they were drying. Evidently the man had been plaguing the neighborhood for quite some time. They let him have it, fists flying. Perhaps because of reactions like this, theft was extremely rare.

There was also a brotherhood among men in Egypt that astounded me. I saw it for the first time when I was in a taxi, a decrepit dented Lada with windows that didn't roll up and oil-stained seats that weren't secured to the floor. It was an infernal summer day and I was sitting next to the driver. (Men always ride in the front with the driver so as not to make him feel like a driver. Drivers prefer to be called chauffeurs.) My "chauffeur" was eating an ice cream—two scoops on a biscuit cone—with obvious pride and delight. He noticed me looking at it and offered me a lick, which I declined. I thought he was merely being polite. It's rude in Egypt (and across the Arab world) to eat in front of other people without offering to share. Shortly afterward, however, we stopped at a busy intersection manned by a traffic policeman in a tattered white uniform. He'd obviously been on the street all day sipping exhaust fumes. He looked completely spent. My chauffeur leaned out the car window and handed the policeman his ice cream. The policeman smiled, took a modest lick, passed back the cone and waved us on our way. It was typical of the generosity I witnessed from people, most of whom couldn't even afford shoes. Instead, they wore plastic flip-flops, known in colloquial Egyptian, as in English, by an onomatopoeia, pronounced *ship-ship*. I was often invited for home-style meals that gave me explosive diarrhea, taken to meet sheikhs who tried to convert me to Islam and dragged to even more fetid neighborhoods than Sahafiyeen to smile in front of people I didn't know (always distant relatives of friends and neighbors), who fed me stewed fava beans straight from dented aluminum pots, mountains of lentils, grilled livers, and sausages stuffed with meat and rice, much of which made me run for the toilet only to gag in horror at what I found there. But I consoled myself with the cliché "It's the thought that counts."

After about eight months in Sahafiyeen the fog in my head began to clear and my stomach started to settle. I could even drink water straight from the tap. All the drinking water in Cairo comes straight from the Nile River, which is so polluted by local industries that it shimmers like oil along certain stretches close to the banks, and it tastes like swimming-pool water because of all the chlorine the government adds to kill germs. There's a local joke that Egyptians can digest rocks. After eight months, I could have at least digested pebbles. And I had begun to speak reasonable Arabic.

Once I began to learn the language, however, I discovered that much of what the people around me were saying was quite disturbing. At the time, there was a scandal widely publicized in the local newspapers involving a group of boys and girls who'd been discovered in the countryside having a wild party that bordered on a mass orgy. The police, local sheikhs and many furious parents had demanded an explanation for the debauchery. It became a shocking national indignity in a country that prides itself on the piety of its people, especially in rural areas. The families of the boys and girls involved in the sex romp concluded that the lapse in morals was brought about because the youngsters had allegedly been chewing bubble gum made in Israel. The newspapers said it had been a plot by the Mossad, Israel's equivalent of the CIA. The newspapers postulated that the Mossad had impregnated the gum with an aphrodisiac as part of an Israeli mission to corrupt Egyptian morals, destroy the fabric of society and thereby weaken the enemy. I found it difficult to believe that everyone I knew accepted the story, but most of them did.

"That's typical of how Jews operate," one of them explained. "Haven't you seen what they're doing in Palestine?"

I thought that I was living in a pocket of ignorance and gullibility. Over the years, however, hardly a day has gone by when I am not presented with a Jewish conspiracy, including the widespread belief that Jews were responsible for the attacks against the Pentagon and World Trade Center in September 2001. After a while, I could start to predict how people in Egypt would explain events through this paranoid paradigm. Conspiracy-driven philosophies are so convincing because they can explain everything without offering any evidence.

I have since had many discussions with Muslim intellectuals who emphatically deny that anti-Semitism is as pervasive in the Arab world as it appeared to me. The most common answer has been that Muslim tradition respects Jews and reveres Moses as a prophet. While this is true, it doesn't explain the complete obsession and mistrust, not only of Israelis but of Jews in general, that is so prominent in Arab society.

As I talked to my friends and neighbors in Cairo, I became regularly involved in discussions about Iraq. The UN sanctions and "double standard" regarding US policy toward Israel were always brought up. People simply couldn't understand why the United States failed to rebuke Israel for what they believed was its clear violation of UN Security Council resolutions, but punished Iraq when it did the same. They had a point. I never heard any blame cast at Saddam Hussein's feet, however. People in Egypt told me they didn't especially like Saddam, but that the main problem Iraq faced came from the United States, not the Iraqi government.

"Millions of Iraqi children are starving every year because of the sanctions!" I remember an impassioned man telling me as I sat in an open-air café in Cairo sipping *sahlab*, a hot milky drink flavored with dried coconut flakes and ground roasted peanuts, and smoking apple-flavored tobacco in a loudly bubbling water pipe. He was furious and slammed his fist on the small, square metal-topped table where we sat. "The Iraqi people can barely eat! They don't have pencils for their schools or medicine in their hospitals! The United States wants Iraq's oil, and if they can't have it they'll punish the Iraqi people!" This was in 1997.

But all my *sahlab* and apple-flavored tobacco cost money—as much as 60 cents for both. After six months in Cairo, I was running low on cash and not moving quickly down the journalist's path. I approached the *Middle East Times*, a local English-language newspaper, and begged for work. The weekly was small, feisty, and like the *Washington Times*, owned by the Moonies, although the group didn't interfere editorially. The paper had earned a reputation for pursuing hard-hitting local stories about corruption, nepotism, vote rigging and police brutality. Opportunity struck when the newspaper's publisher sacked the editor in chief without warning or preamble. The newspaper's entire staff, quite nobly I must say, walked out in solidarity. Although I was uncomfortable about being a scab, I stepped into the newspaper's office in a residential apartment in Cairo and assumed the roles of editor in chief, sole reporter, copy editor and layout designer. The weekly's quality inevitably dipped under my inexperienced stewardship, but I never missed an issue. There were ample spelling errors and factual mistakes, but I did my best and slowly rebuilt the staff, settling into the role of news editor.

During this period, I also found myself drawn to write about the Muslim Brotherhood, an influential Egypt-based Islamic group, and the more violent Muslim fundamentalist organizations *al-Jamaa al-Islamiya* ("the Islamic Group") and *al-Jihad*, led by Ayman al-Zawahiri, deputy to al-Qaeda leader Osama bin Laden. The Muslim Brotherhood, founded in 1928, is officially banned in Egypt. The government, however, tolerates the group while keeping a watchful eye on the group's leaders (perhaps not coincidentally, the symbol of Egypt's intelligence agency is an open, all-seeing Pharaonic–style eye), frequently imprisoning them. The Muslim Brotherhood is arguably the most important Islamic political organization in the Middle East, and many militant Islamic fundamentalist groups have links (usually indirect) or historical ties to the Brotherhood.

Over the next few years, I branched out and began writing articles for various newspapers and magazines and I was able to eke out a tolerable income by Egyptian standards. I was about to discover, however, that the Egyptian government was uncomfortable with my deepening interest in Islamic militant groups. I learned that my telephone was tapped, albeit crudely. One day I picked up the receiver and could hear a conversation in the background. Several men were laughing and coughing. I could also hear a clinking sound. As soon as I began to speak, the conversation went silent and I was given a dial tone. I didn't think much of it until I started consistently hearing the same voices, the same hacking coughs and, more often, that same clinking sound. A few weeks later, while at a coffee shop drinking tea, it became clear to me what the sound was. The men were stirring sugar in their glasses of tea.

Soon after suspecting my phone was bugged, I was followed. I'd just returned from a weekend trip to Alexandria and was buying a magazine from a vendor displaying dozens of week-old foreign periodicals spread out on the sidewalk when a security agent (obvious in the black leather trench coat he wore) approached me and asked me if I'd enjoyed my lunch at Alexandria's Greek Club and the whisky I'd swilled at the Havana Bistro, two restaurants I'd visited in the Mediterranean city. I told him that I had and jokingly suggested that he join me on my next weekend jaunt. I told the agent that I'd stayed at the Metropole Hotel, a wonderfully renovated establishment near Alexandria's old train station. He could get an adjacent room, I suggested. The agent said coldly that he was fully aware of where I'd stayed. This was petty intimidation and it didn't bother me much at the time.

The government's interference only turned menacing when I wrote an article in 1997 for Reuters describing how Muslim militants were extorting money from Coptic Christians in southern Egypt by demanding that they pay *jizia*, an ancient tax Muslim rulers once extracted from non-Muslims in lieu of military service. The article hit a nerve. The Egyptian government is highly sensitive about relations between Muslims and Christians in the country. The government denies accusations that it discriminates against Christians and fears any press reports that might provide fuel to Egypt's detractors. My story provoked a string of similar articles, including one in the *Los Angeles Times*. The article was also used by Coptic lobby groups in the United States as evidence of prejudice against Christians. Christian interest groups reprinted the story in their brochures and posted it on the Internet. A friend of mine in Egypt's powerful *Amm al-Dowla*, or State Security Service, told me that US congressmen raised the issue of discrimination against Christians and referred directly to my article in a meeting with Egypt's President Hosni Mubarak during a visit to Washington. According to my source, Mubarak ordered the security agencies to find out who I was. The Egyptian security services suspected that I might have been a CIA agent and that the article I wrote was designed to undercut Mubarak during his trip to Washington. Shortly after Mubarak's return, an Egyptian tabloid, *al-Hakika*—"The Truth"—which, like all newspapers in Egypt, was heavily influenced by the government, printed a front-page article denouncing me as a spy. RICHARD ENGEL, THE DIRECTOR OF THE CIA STATION IN EGYPT, HAS BEEN ARRESTED BY THE SECURITY SERVICES! ran the banner headline, printed in red to make sure nobody missed it. I called a senior official at the US embassy and indicated that the article was a problem for me. My radical Muslim confidants were already excruciatingly paranoid and apt to see conspiracy theories everywhere. It had taken me more than two years to build their trust and dismiss initial assumptions that I worked for the CIA and/or the Mossad. This stupid article put my life in danger! The US embassy official, in typical fashion, said he could do nothing for me unless I was arrested. Over the years I've noticed a consistent reluctance on the part of US embassy staff in the Middle East to leave their fortress-like compounds and dirty their hands by mingling with locals or local politics. I can understand their desire to stay above the confusing fray, but the embassy's self-imposed isolation contributes to the fact that American policy in the Middle East has often come across as disconnected from the realities and prevalent sentiments in the region.

Despite the article, I continued to work. I tried to reassure one of my best contacts, a lawyer for the *Jamaa Islamiya*, a group that has killed scores of tourists in Egypt in very unpleasant ways, that the accusation was baseless slander. I defended myself by arguing that *al-Hakika* had often printed lies about the *Jamaa Islamiya*. I asked him why, therefore, did he believe the tabloid when it wrote articles about me? It's common in Arab culture to use rhetorical questions to make an argument. My contact seemed to buy it, and I was satisfied that I was no longer in immediate danger.

I later learned from my security source that the *Amm al-Dowla* (the dreaded branch of the interior ministry infamous for using torture to extract information, including applying electric shocks to prisoners' genitals and nipples and hanging them by their arms tied behind their backs) had planted the article to test me. If I'd fled the country, it would have evidently proven that I did in fact work for the CIA. Since I stayed, I was in the clear, my source told me.

But soon thereafter I took a job in Jerusalem with the English service of the French News Agency. I was delighted to have the opportunity to see the Middle East from the opposite side of the political spectrum—for years, I'd been hearing what Israelis were like from Arabs—and I was also excited because in late 1999, it seemed that a new era of peace between Israelis and Palestinians was dawning.

Jerusalem was bubbling with enthusiasm when I arrived, and I fully expected to be writing stories about the birth of Palestine and the forging of new relations between two neighboring countries: one Arab, one Jewish. Instead, I found myself covering the *Al-Aqsa Intifada*, splitting time between gun battles in the West Bank and Gaza Strip and walking through the grisly aftermath of suicide bombings across Israel.

CHAPTER TWO

I WAS SIPPING COFFEE in my apartment in Jerusalem in February 2001, an empty notebook and a pile of newspapers in front of me, trying to figure out what the landslide victory of life-long right winger Ariel Sharon over Labor Party leader Ehud Barak in Israel's prime ministerial election meant for the prospect of a negotiated peace deal in the Middle East when I learned that the new US president, George W. Bush, had ordered the most penetrating military strikes against Iraq in three years. Less than one month after taking office, President Bush had authorized more than twenty aircraft to destroy Iraqi radar targets, including sites outside of the no-fly zones in northern and southern Iraq for the first time since 1998's Operation Desert Fox—four days of air strikes launched by President Bill Clinton after UN weapons inspectors left Iraq complaining of the government's lack of cooperation. President Bush told reporters that the latest raid was designed both to send a message to Saddam Hussein that the United States would not tolerate his country's building weapons of mass destruction and to degrade Iraq's capability to threaten US and British planes patrolling the no-fly zones enacted after the 1991 Gulf War to protect Kurds in northern Iraq and Shiite Muslims in the South from Iraqi air assaults.

Arab nations promptly accused the Bush administration of focusing on Iraq instead of on the five months of intense Israeli-Palestinian bloodshed, which in Arab opinion was the top priority in the Middle East. Arab sentiment was especially strong because of televised coverage of the Palestinian uprising, or intifada, and Israel's often aggressive countermeasures. From Morocco to Iraq, people were glued to television sets like never before, becoming active spectators to the conflict like sports fans. I remember walking through the old medina of the Moroccan city of Fez—scattering baksheesh around me like grain to keep away the freelance teenage guides who refused to let me lose myself in the labyrinth of narrow alleys and passageways that zigzagged through the ancient city—when I came across a crowd of people in front of the glass window of a store selling television sets. I squeezed among the pack to see what was so interesting and was somewhat surprised to see so many people watching the news. They were watching al-Jazeera, which could only be seen with a satellite dish. Since most people couldn't afford to have a dish at home, they watched al-Jazeera through the store window instead. The previous Palestinian intifada in the late 1980s had been televised, but not live. Before al-Jazeera, Arab television consisted almost entirely of government-controlled broadcasts that packaged news into recorded segments for a few daily bulletins. Arab state-run television was also painfully dry, always leading broadcasts with reports about the nation's ruler, no matter how trivial. With the advent of al-Jazeera, Arabs were given their first taste of live television: dramatic events unfolding twenty-four hours a day. Al-Jazeera also had flashy graphics, interviewed controversial Arab opinion makers and even had a correspondent in Israel. When I visited al-Jazeera's ultramodern newsroom in the Qatari capital, Doha, later that year I sensed energy. Most of the journalists were young, hard-working and savvy, totally unlike the tired employees I'd met at behemoth state television networks I'd visited in Yemen and Egypt operating out of government ministry buildings. Al-Jazeera had been broadcasting since 1996, but until the outbreak of the intifada there hadn't been a major story of mass Arab interest, especially one with such powerful pictures. With the outbreak of the second intifada in September 2000, al-Jazeera broadcast streams of virtually uncut footage of Palestinian children throwing stones and Israeli soldiers shooting and demolishing homes. The pictures al-Jazeera broadcast were also considerably more graphic than those shown on the Western networks.

In April 2001, Prime Minister Sharon ordered his army for the first time to seize land governed by Yasser Arafat's Palestinian Authority under the terms of peace accords worked out since 1993. In May, a Palestinian suicide bomber killed five Israelis in a shopping mall in the Israeli coastal city of Netanya, triggering an Israeli bombardment of Palestinian Authority headquarters in the Gaza Strip with US-made F-16 fighter jets, the first time the weapon had been used in the Palestinian territories since the 1967 Middle East war. In June, a Palestinian suicide bomber killed nearly two dozen Israelis, most of them teenagers, at a seafront discotheque in Tel Aviv. In July, Israeli forces killed eight Palestinians during a rocket attack against Hamas leaders in the northern West Bank city of Nablus. A month later, yet another suicide bomber blew up a pizzeria in downtown Jerusalem. An Israeli opinion poll at the time reflected that the majority of Israelis felt that Sharon—the retired general most Arabs held responsible for the massacre of hundreds of Palestinian civilians by pro-Israeli Christian militias in Lebanon in 1982—was being too soft on the Palestinians. Attitudes in the Arab world also were hardening.

By August 2001, the most popular song in the Arab world was a catchy tune with the point-blank title "I Hate Israel." The vitriolic jingle became a fixture at weddings throughout the Middle East, where belly dancers would gyrate to its Arab-pop beat. Judging by the song's popularity, the blunt sentiment it expressed was shared by millions of Arabs. "I Hate Israel" was not a hit, however, with McDonald's, and the hamburger chain dropped the man behind the smash single, singer Shaaban Abdel Rahim, as the pitchman for the new McFalafel sandwich.

I first heard "I Hate Israel" in the front seat of a taxi in Cairo I assumed would crash before taking me to the Arab League, where I was supposed to report on a meeting of government ministers; the problem with taxi drivers in Cairo is that they believe too deeply in destiny. The taxi driver was blaring the song, honking to its beat, as he raced through Cairo's frenetic traffic with such blatant disregard for driving norms that even other daredevil Cairenes, known for laughing in the face of traffic laws, were taken aback by his ability to squeeze between speeding cars, stop instantly, accelerate through red lights and turn without warning. I'd never heard of Shaaban Abdel Rahim and was surprised by the directness of the lyrics; he belted out "I Hate Israel" over and over. I asked the driver who the singer was. The driver pulled the car to a screeching halt, reached between my legs and pulled the cassette's box from under my seat. The driver told me Shaaban Abdel Rahim had formerly been a *makwagi*, a man who ironed clothing for a living, and that he'd become an overnight success with "I Hate Israel." The driver liked Abdel Rahim because of his *shaabi* background and because he had the courage to say what many Arabs were thinking, unlike Arab governments attending the Arab League meeting.

The next day I was surprised to discover, however, that the hit movie that summer in Egypt was *Days of Sadat,* a fictionalized biography of Egypt's late president Anwar Sadat, who made peace with Israel. I watched the movie from the grand balcony of a theater that must have been gorgeous in the 1960s but was now somewhat worn around the edges, with torn seats and stained carpeting that curled up at door jambs. The film, which, like all movies in Egypt, was subject to the scrutiny and approval of the state censor, lionized the former Egyptian leader and praised his decision in 1979 to sign a peace treaty with Israel, though it would eventually cost him his life. Sadat was assassinated in 1981 by Islamic extremists opposed to his crackdown on their activities and for making peace with Israel.

I asked a respected Egyptian sociologist, Gamal Abdel Gawad, from the al-Ahram Center for Political and Strategic Studies, to explain the apparent paradox of Egypt's hit song and the summer blockbuster. Gawad said Egyptians were going through one of the most dramatic shifts in public opinion in recent history because of the fighting in the West Bank and Gaza Strip. Egyptians, he said, were losing faith in the peace they'd reached with Israel and *Days of Sadat* was an attempt to reassure the public that it had made the correct decision to bury the hatchet two decades ago. He said Egyptians were realistic and didn't want another war with Israel, but desperately hoped the United States would do more to pressure Sharon.

Then came the September 11 attacks in New York and Washington and the war in Afghanistan. Attention shifted away from the Israeli-Palestinian crisis for a few months, but the fighting didn't cease. In fact, it was about to get much worse.

In January 2002, a twenty-year-old Palestinian woman became the first-ever female suicide bomber. In February, Sharon told an Israeli newspaper that he regretted not eliminating

Arafat in Lebanon two decades earlier. A peace plan forwarded by Saudi Arabia's Crown Prince Abdullah that offered normal relations between Israel and all of the Arab world in exchange for lands captured in the 1967 Middle East war died on the vine.

Israeli-Palestinian fighting took a dramatic turn for the worse in March with a savage suicide bombing during a Jewish Passover meal. Two dozen people were killed when the bomber, a former employee at the hotel in Netanya, burst into the dining room where families were celebrating the holiday ritual. The attack triggered a massive Israeli offensive, Operation Defensive Shield, which saw the Israeli army reoccupy nearly all of the major Palestinian towns and cities on the West Bank over the next two months. The army also confined Arafat to his West Bank headquarters in Ramallah. Palestinian gunmen barricaded themselves in Bethlehem's Church of the Nativity. It was a tumultuous several months, broadcast live on al-Jazeera and its up-and-coming competitor Abu Dhabi. No one in the Arab world was thinking about Iraq at the time, but the Bush administration seemed to be reading from a different Middle East book. In January, Bush declared Iraq to be part of his "axis of evil," along with Iran and North Korea.

"Bush and Sharon are the axis of evil!" Palestinian protesters chanted across the West Bank and the Gaza Strip, their message beamed into households across the Middle East.

In September 2002, President Bush called on the United Nations to take action against Iraq. People in the Arab world didn't know why the US administration was suddenly picking on Iraq. Inspectors arrived in Baghdad a month later to monitor Iraqi disarmament. Over the next several months, the United States rejected Iraq's 12,000-page explanation of its banned weapons programs and inspectors searched Iraq without finding any "smoking guns." The United States and Britain also began deploying troops to the region and it seemed to many pundits that the countdown to war had begun. Shaaban Abdel Rahim had another hit across the Arab world entitled "The Attack on Iraq."

"You've inspected Iraq, now go inspect Israel!" crooned the paunchy singer, who since his success with "I Hate Israel" had developed a penchant for gold watches (he wore several at a time), red blazers and inky-black silk shirts. His taste and style was something of an embarrassment to the elite in the Arab world, but with his new song, the former *makwagi* had again captured the prevailing mood in the Arab world.

"Enough!" sang Shaaban. "Chechnya! Afghanistan! Palestine! Southern Lebanon! The Golan [Heights]! And now Iraq too?! It's too much for people. Shame on you! Enough, enough, enough!"

I was in Jerusalem when the UN inspectors returned to Iraq, trying to figure out how I could get to Baghdad in case the war did happen. I wasn't convinced at the time that it would. A war with Iraq seemed to fly too much in the face of the prevailing sentiment in the already boiling Arab world.

But getting into Iraq wasn't easy. A reporter's visa was

nearly impossible to obtain. The Iraqi Information Ministry was limiting the number of foreign journalists in the country. For years, the Iraqi government used a system of minders to control the flow of information coming out of the country. The Information Ministry—through the press center run at the time by Uday al-Ta'e—assigned each major newspaper reporter or television crew a minder. They were all Iraqi intelligence officers. It was the minders' job to accompany reporters when they traveled around Iraq, encourage them to do stories favorable to the Iraqi government and write nasty reports about the journalists who refused to do so. It was a labor-intensive system, and the Information Ministry simply couldn't handle too many reporters at any given time, especially during such a sensitive period as the buildup to a possible war. The more reporters in Iraq, the less the government could control each one. Iraq was counting on positive press to help avert military action. Visa controls were therefore especially strict. Iraq ultimately decided to give each major news outlet only one, or occasionally two, reporting visas. Perhaps it goes without saying that correspondents fought tooth and nail against each other and jockeyed hard within their organizations to get their hands on those visas. Many friendships among reporters were destroyed by pettiness, greed, overarching ambition and backstabbing during this period.

In Jerusalem, I'd become a freelance correspondent for ABC, mainly reporting for the overnight programs *World News Now* and *World News This Morning* and for the New York affiliate. I had a strong relationship with ABC, but was nowhere near the top of the network's list of correspondents to receive a prized reporting visa for Iraq. In fact, I was not even in the running. I would have to do it myself.

I had visited Iraq on a two-week reporting trip in October 2002 to cover Saddam Hussein's referendum, the election in which not a single Iraqi supposedly voted against Saddam's continued, unchallenged and brutal rule. Although the vote was obviously preordained, the Iraqi Information Ministry had considered the event to be an opportunity to show the international community the Iraqi people's profound love for their "father" Saddam Hussein. The Information Ministry had issued hundreds of reporting visas ahead of the referendum, including one to me, working at the time for *The World*, a public radio show based in Boston. I made several contacts during my initial visit and left $200 "facilitation fees" with low-level officials of the Information Ministry's press center, which I hoped would assure success with future visa applications. As tension mounted, however, the money I'd left proved worthless. By January 2003, the front door to Iraq was closed.

Every day there was new speculation about the start date of the possible military campaign. I believed that if the war were to happen, it would not begin until after the *hajj,* the annual Muslim pilgrimage to the holy cities of Mecca and Medina, which in 2003 fell in mid-February. I assumed the Saudis, the United States' most influential Arab ally, would not want a war to be under way while roughly a million and a half Muslims were crowded in the kingdom. I calculated that the war might begin sometime after the hajj and before the onset of the intense summer heat in Iraq that starts in June. My goal was to be in position in Baghdad by the first week of March.

From Jerusalem I telephoned a female Jordanian friend. Although she shall remain nameless, I can describe her as a flamboyant, stylish, melodramatic shopaholic, capable of swerving from exuberant joy to demonic rage with the explosive speed of a Ferrari. She suggested that I enter Iraq as a peace activist. The visas issued to peace activists were the same as those for journalists, with the critical difference that on each one it was written that it had been issued by the Iraqi Peace and Friendship Society, an arm of the Iraqi government that brought foreigners to the country to be human shields. The organization imported dozens of peaceniks, do-gooders, career hippies, Muslim fundamentalists and assorted protesters and housed them at oil refineries, power plants, air force bases and other strategic sites in the hopes that their presence would dissuade the United States from attacking them. I had no interest in becoming a human shield, especially in defense of Saddam Hussein, but faced with no better option, I went for it.

My Jordanian friend put me in touch with one of her contacts at the Iraqi embassy in Amman and told me to butter him up.

I decided to travel via London and stock up on supplies, including baby clothing and a few boxes of expensive tea, treats I'd exchange for favors. While it's unfair to stereotype,

Arabs generally drink enormous quantities of tea. Baby clothing is also always a good bribe, provided the intended mark
has children. My mark, the Iraqi official at the embassy in
Amman directly responsible for issuing visas, had a three-
year-old son on whom he doted. I bought him a formal little
suit from Mothercare in London. The purpose behind my
generosity was to convince him to issue me the human shield
visa without overly scrutinizing my passport. It would have
been very easy for him to discover that I was a reporter
because it was written in Arabic on several stamps in my
passport. The gifts evidently did the trick, because I was
issued a peace activist visa on the spot on the day I arrived in
Amman.

Peace activists didn't travel, however, with the gear I
wanted to bring to Baghdad, including $20,000 in cash, a bul-
letproof jacket, a chemical/biological/radiological suit and gas
mask, injectors of atropine (an antidote for nerve agent), a
handheld video camera and a satellite telephone. I would have
to smuggle them in.

There were two ways to travel from Amman to Baghdad: a
ten-hour drive overland or a direct hour-long flight. I chose to
go by auto, even though it was the more uncomfortable and
precarious route. The only road to Baghdad from Jordan is a
highway that cuts straight through Iraq's Western Desert. Bandits were known to raid cars on the road, a problem that dramatically worsened after the war. The paved road was also completely flat and almost entirely without curves. The monotony of
the journey had lulled more than a few drivers to sleep at the

wheel. I chose to drive, however, because I thought there would be more room to hide the equipment in the large GMC Suburbans that made the cross-border hegira. There were fewer customs, intelligence and other Iraqi officials at the land border than at the airport.

I set off in the middle of the night on March 5, armed with $20,000 wrapped in a pouch shaped like an Ace bandage around my ankle, my pockets bloated with $20 bills (it's important to have small notes because you can't ask for change when making a payoff), a car filled with illicit equipment, a misleading visa and no firm commitment from ABC. I was in a fairly weak position, all things considered.

The GMC Suburban was a huge white gas guzzler with red racing stripes painted down the sides. There were two pictures taped to the back windows: one of Saddam Hussein, the other of Jordan's King Abdullah II. The vehicle was also loaded with every imaginable gadget, doodad and bric-a-brac known to bad taste. The well between the driver and passenger seats was cluttered with a two-cup cup holder, an ashtray overflowing with cigarette butts, a coffeemaker and a mini television set attached to a DVD player. Every time the driver turned the ignition key a digitized voice recited a verse from the Koran. It was a classy ride.

My driver, a Jordanian man of about thirty named Sami, told me he did the commute from Amman to Baghdad three times a week. I'd been told that Sami could be trusted, but I didn't know him personally. I kept our conversation limited to ramblings about the weather, food and women, the best subjects to discuss when trying to kill time without revealing anything.

Sami popped in a DVD, one of two he had with him. The first was a medley of Arabic pop music videos, mostly men with mustaches standing by swimming pools crooning love songs. The other was of Jennifer Lopez videos, which seemed to me to be very risqué. Sami kept stealing peeks at J-Lo instead of watching the road. I did too. I warned him that I didn't want death by Lopez.

Both DVDs were hopelessly scratched. They skipped constantly, although Sami didn't seem to notice and just let them play, skipping and repeating until I lashed out in a burst of frustration and stopped them.

At about four-thirty in the morning we arrived at the Iraqi border. It was best to travel through the desert on the way to Baghdad at first light, before too many bandits woke up.

Sami easily cleared us through Iraqi customs, palming money left and right to Iraqi officials. He handed out so many packets of Marlboros that he looked as though he worked for Philip Morris. I'd given Sami a stack of twenties as we pulled up to the border. He'd told me Iraqis didn't like to take bribes in their own currency, the dinar, because the notes were so big and bulky they made an outline that was obvious in their pockets. Ten dollars' worth of dinars, for example, was a bundle of notes about an inch thick.

Suddenly Sami rushed back to the car, opened the passenger side door and urgently whispered to me: "You don't speak Arabic."

"Why?" I asked.

"An Iraqi intelligence agent is coming with us to Baghdad."

I understood that this was one of many favors necessary to smooth my passage through the border with my unregistered equipment.

I offered the intelligence agent the front seat, which he accepted. I stretched out in the back, but because my adrenaline was up I couldn't sleep. Instead, I sat in awkward silence pretending not to speak Arabic. There was so much that I wanted to ask.

The Iraqi desert looked bleak: miles and miles of unbroken sand and scrub. Occasionally we passed military bases along the road. I feigned disinterest to avoid raising the suspicion of the intelligence officer, who never introduced himself. We passed through a dense palm grove as we crossed the Euphrates River and eventually arrived at a military checkpoint outside Baghdad. The guard waved us through after Sami handed him a single 250-dinar note, worth roughly nine cents.

We parked the GMC at a lot in the al-Mansour neighborhood, where I loaded my gear into a local taxi and started hunting for a hotel.

The most famous hotel at the time was the Al-Rashid, the most luxurious in town and where most of the journalists were staying. It was relatively expensive, about $150 a night, and I wanted to conserve my cash for an emergency. The Al-Rashid was also famously packed to the brim with Iraqi intelligence officers. I didn't want to stay at the Al-Rashid until I sorted out my visa situation. My plan was to convert my human shield visa into a reporting visa.

I asked a local driver in purposely broken Arabic to find me a small clean hotel, somewhere outside the center of town. I wanted to be anonymous at this stage, the "gray man," unseen until my paperwork was in order.

We eventually arrived at the Flowers Land Hotel, a small, family-run establishment on a narrow side street. My room was a mini apartment with a kitchen, a living room and two small bedrooms. It also had two balconies that faced southeast, which would be convenient for my satellite phone.

Surprisingly, I didn't sense any tension in the air in Baghdad when I first arrived. I saw a steady flow of traffic in the streets. Stores were open and appeared to be full of customers and merchandise. I didn't have a sense that Iraq was on the verge of war.

It was early evening by the time I was settled into the hotel room. I switched on Iraqi state television and watched for a couple of hours. The news broadcasts were full of reports about international opposition to the war and global anti-war protests.

I telephoned a low-ranking official from the press center named Kazem who'd been recommended to me in Jordan. I hoped he would be able to help me register at the press center and sort out my visa dilemma.

Kazem was cautious and vague over the telephone. I understood that he was most likely worried that the hotel's phone—or even more likely his home phone—was bugged. I was also certain that at least one of the lines was tapped. That was part of the reason I wanted to discuss my visa dilemma over the telephone. I assumed it was better to let the intelligence service know that I was really a journalist breaking the rules than to have them actually suspect me of being a spy. This is the way people used to think in Baghdad. It was a completely paranoid existence. Over the years I've come to assume many phones in the Arab world, especially at hotels, are tapped. But I don't know how effective it is. A dear diplomat friend—who after many glasses of scotch one night in Cairo finally confirmed my suspicion that he worked for the intelligence service of an Eastern European country—told me that I needn't worry too much about talking on a bugged phone in most Arab countries. He said that his experience in Eastern Europe had shown him that intelligence agencies in developing countries tape many conversations, but that they do not have the technical or human capacity to effectively deal with all the data they collect. They don't have time to sort through reels and reels of audio tape or process the information, especially if the conversations are in a foreign language. He recommended, however, that I always avoid saying the name of the nation's president, which could ring out in the middle of a conversation and alert eavesdroppers.

Kazem promised to drop by my hotel in the morning, and I flipped on the television before turning in for the night. I watched an Arab variety show on Egypt's Dream TV, a new private satellite channel. The guest that night was Shaaban

Abdel Rahim performing his hit "The Attack on Iraq," in obvious lip sync.

"Do you want to divide Iraq? What do you want exactly?
Honestly, do you have your eyes on Iraq's oil?" he sang. "Iraq,
after Afghanistan, nobody knows whose turn will come next."

CHAPTER THREE

I'VE OFTEN BEEN ASKED what the most frightening moment of the second Gulf War was. For me (and I believe for most of the journalists in Iraq and certainly their editors) the period immediately preceding the actual fighting was the most psychologically taxing. No one knew what the Pentagon would unleash against Iraq or how the country would react. There had been a plethora of speculative media reports and punditry forecasting that the US air campaign would make World War II, let alone the first Gulf War, look toothless by comparison. It also had been widely reported that "Shock and Awe," as military planners in Washington had so ominously dubbed the military phase, might see the use of such behemoth weapons as the Massive Ordnance Air Blast (MOAB), affectionately nicknamed the "Mother of All Bombs"—a 21,000-pound leviathan, the biggest conventional bomb in the US military arsenal. There'd also been leaks that the US military was considering using so-called e-bombs to knock out Iraqi computers and communication equipment, making it nearly impossible for the Iraqi army to control its forces. The microwave pulse supposedly emitted by the top secret e-bombs also would have, presumably, fried the laptop computers, satellite telephones and video uplinks on which foreign journalists relied. Why risk staying in Baghdad if we couldn't report on what we were seeing? Furthermore, no one knew how the Iraqi people would react to tanks storming through the capital, or even more troubling, how the Iraqi regime would act during its death throes. Would the government seize Westerners (especially Americans) or use chemical or biological weapons? Would Saddam Hussein's henchmen round up all the Americans and kill one every hour until the bombings stopped? It was like knowing a train was coming and I was standing on the tracks. Although I chose to stay in Baghdad, I certainly understood why other reporters and editors decided to pull out when the fighting seemed imminent. Oddly, once the bombs started falling I actually felt a bizarre sense of relief. It was like the train had come down the tracks, hit me and I'd survived.

The psychological strain of the countdown to war and the endless speculation also weighed heavily on the Iraqi people, although most were too scared of their government to show it.

I had breakfast in the lobby of the Flowers Land Hotel, drumming my fingers on the table as I waited anxiously for Kazem, the press center fixer, to arrive and help me change my visa status. Conducting interviews with the wrong visa would have landed me in jail.

The breakfast was not an exotic Arabian feast but something one might have expected to be served at a Soviet-era youth hostel: prepackaged white-bread rolls, very gelatinous strawberry jelly, hard-boiled eggs and weak tea. Sadly, I've found this type of bottom-end Western cuisine to be common in many Arab urban sprawls. In Yemen—in my opinion the most exquisite country in the Arab world, with its mud buildings covered in white plaster and stained glass windows—many people start the day with a sandwich of yellow Kraft cheese and jelly. I found it to be a sad by-product of globalization.

Over breakfast that morning I read *Babel*, the Iraqi Arabic-language daily newspaper owned by Saddam's eldest son—the famously violent rapist Uday—and Iraq's own English-language newspaper, the *Iraq Daily*. The *Iraq Daily*'s main headline was LEADER PRESIDENT SADDAM HUSSEIN MEETS HIS CABINET. What journalistic prowess. The newspaper's cover prominently featured a photograph of Saddam meeting Iraq's Revolutionary Command Council, Saddam's personal gaggle of sycophants. The photograph was a standard shot of Saddam sitting at a long table flanked by his cowering advisors in green uniforms. Many of the articles in the *Iraq Daily*, which were more like editorials, argued that world opinion was opposed to the US and British threats of war. The newspaper even highlighted the support for Saddam Hussein by a group it referred to as the "Radical Serbian Party." I wonder if it gave the Iraqi people any solace knowing that the radical Serbs were poised to save the day.

Hours passed without any word from Kazem. I couldn't call him because there was no mobile phone network in Iraq. I was surprised to discover, however, that there was an Internet connection at the hotel's business center—a bare white room with two computers supervised by a twenty-one-year-old hacker named Mohammed. Mohammed, who had jet-black hair puffed into a slight bouffant, proudly explained how he'd managed to beat the Iraqi censors.

Very few Iraqis had Internet connections in their homes. In fact, it had been illegal for anyone without a Ph.D. to have one. The vast majority of Iraqis who wanted to explore the Web or send e-mail therefore used business centers (referred to in the Arab world as "business*men* centers") in hotels, universities or professional syndicates. As I trolled the Web that day, I discovered that the Iraqi government had blocked sites containing information about Iraqi opposition groups, pornography and, most significant, all portals that provided free Web-based e-mail like Hotmail and Yahoo. Mohammed said Iraqi authorities blocked Web-based e-mail sites because they couldn't monitor them. Iraq was a closed society and the government obviously didn't want its people to have too much unregulated contact with the outside world. The only way for Iraqis to send e-mail was through accounts linked to the Iraqi government's Internet service provider (ISP), which could easily be opened.

Mohammed, however, spent hours each day scouring the

Web for sites that offered free e-mail that the censors didn't know about. He had a list of about fifteen different sites that weren't yet on the government's radar.

Mohammed was somewhat of a braggart about his ability to get around the censors and use computers, but not without reason. At thirteen, he'd stolen money from his father's bureau to buy his first computer. He'd taught himself to write programs and knew how to tap into the server of the nearby Russian consulate. Mohammed signed me up for a free e-mail account based in Moldova. It gave me a secure way to communicate with my family, friends and editors until power and phone lines were cut in the later stages of the war.

There were several other journalists staying at the Flowers Land Hotel from Russia, France and Japan. Like me, they were all feverishly debating when—for some even if—the war would begin. Some journalists said they expected the fighting to start very soon. Everyone acted as if he or she had secret information. Most journalists expected that the Iraqi government would round up all the foreigners in the country (almost exclusively reporters at this stage) and corral them in a central location to serve as human shields. Ironically, I'd have ended up as a human shield no matter what kind of visa I had. Where we would be taken and what exactly would happen to us was the subject of hot debates discussed in hushed tones. I wasn't sure that I wanted to allow myself to be taken, and I checked my room for places to hide should a soft knock come on the door in the middle of the night (secret police in the Arab world are said to always knock softly so as not to tempt people to run away). I was on the fifth floor of the hotel, and I was even considering climbing out the window and jumping to the balcony of the empty adjacent room, but this option was so bad it was really no option at all.

Kazem finally arrived at the hotel a few days later and we exchanged kisses on the cheeks according to Arab custom. We sat at a private table in the corner of the dining room. I had a thousand questions I wanted to ask. Kazem, a small bespectacled man who wore a neat three-piece suit, apologized for being incommunicado and told me his mother had suffered a stroke. His delicate hands were trembling as he sipped his tiny cup of Turkish coffee. He'd slept the night by his mother's bedside. Kazem told me it was going to be difficult to change my visa, but promised to raise the issue directly with Uday al-Ta'e. I wasn't optimistic, but it was the best shot I had.

I took advantage of the lull to stock up on supplies and learn anything I could about the mood in Iraq. Finding the right driver was essential and there were several on couches in the hotel lobby, waiting for business. I picked Zafar because at about forty, he was older than the others. I've never trusted young drivers, who I think tend to be too opportunistic. Zafar was heavyset, had a close-cropped beard and was openly greedy. I could sense his cupidity immediately. He wanted to be hired a week at a time and immediately asked me if I'd pay him even for the days we didn't go anywhere together. Although I understood his desire to be on a retainer, it's very unusual in

Arab society to start a relationship—even a business relationship—with a discussion about money. I wasn't overly dis-
turbed by his hunger for cash and wondered if it meant that
I could buy his loyalty. Zafar also had a very dumpy car, a
Volkswagen Passat from 1986 that was manufactured in Brazil
and known locally as a *brazili*. It didn't attract attention,
which I thought was a clear advantage over a flashy Mercedes
or sparkling new GMC Suburban. If a riot erupted or American troops stormed the capital, I thought it would be best to
be in an inconspicuous car. The only problem (aside from the
shredded interior) was that the *brazili* cornered badly and
couldn't make a fast getaway in a pinch.

Zafar and I went on a supply run, buying a gas-powered
electric generator (assuming the power would eventually be
cut), four empty 35-liter jerricans for water, a 35-liter can of
gasoline, 5 liters of oil (for the generator), a case of bottled min-
eral water, a crowbar (in case I needed to pry open a jammed
door or found myself locked inside a building), copper wire (to
extend the antenna of my shortwave radio), canned food (tuna
fish and sardines), a can opener (not to be forgotten!), a flashlight and extra batteries. It was only my first of many supply
runs that would become more specific as my increasingly paranoid mind came up with ever worse scenarios I feared I would
run into. I even bought earplugs, which I thought I might need
during the bombings.

Like many journalists, I'd taken a course in hazardous
environment training, in my case taught by former members

of the British special forces. The basic premise they imparted was to try to maintain as much independence as possible in dangerous situations by doing simple things: Carry your passport, fill the car with gas and stick together with your team. I'd also spent five summers learning, and for the last two years teaching, wilderness survival skills at a camp for children in Wyoming. The experience was useful in teaching me how to improvise, but knowing how to catch a brook trout without a hook wasn't especially helpful in Baghdad.

As I drove around the city with Zafar—which was illegal because I wasn't supposed to be roaming around except with a minder from the press center, which I couldn't get because I wasn't officially registered as a journalist—I was shocked to see how blasé most Iraqis seemed about the prospect of war.

"I don't think the war will happen," Zafar told me as we drove back to the hotel. "I hear the French are going to send in troops to block the war."

"I doubt it," I told him, somewhat surprised—and suspicious—that he was talking to me so openly.

Zafar's thinking didn't seem atypical, however. I sensed no panic in Baghdad despite the fact that there were nearly 200,000 US troops in Kuwait and the American media were busy discussing how awesome and devastating the war would be. I saw Iraqis buying clothing and families strolling down the streets with their children eating ice cream. I saw construction workers building homes. Workers were repaving the driveway in front of the foreign ministry. Street cleaners were sweeping trash off sidewalks. There was a wedding near my hotel with a loud band. As I prepared for bed that night listening to the drums, flutes and ululating women in the wedding party, I imagined what the scene would have been like if the tables were turned and the United States was living under the threat of an imminent war to topple the government. I pictured Americans making massive withdrawals of cash and transferring their savings accounts overseas. I imagined there would have been a crisis in the insurance markets and that people would be digging bomb shelters in their backyards. Sales of Prozac would have gone through the roof. I imagined American television stations providing wall-to-wall coverage, with experts offering advice on how to prepare for war. Iraq couldn't have been more different. The people simply went about their lives as if nothing were wrong. The government couldn't have been happier with this attitude. Panic at this stage could have spelled a premature end for the Iraqi regime.

March 8

Rancid shwarma got to me. It hit my stomach like a rowdy band of thieves who've been making merry in my gut. It struck after I bought Zafar lunch in an attempt to buy his trust. But what a price I'm paying! The chicken shwarma tasted fine, but obviously the fowl was foul. I have a fever, a headache, a queasy stomach, shaky legs and feel somewhat delirious. I bought some vitamin C at pharmacy. I'm going to try to rest as much as possible today.

What I didn't write in my journal was that while I was at the pharmacy I set up the first of many safe houses in Baghdad. Zafar had driven me to the pharmacy, which I was somewhat surprised to find well stocked after years of hearing about medicine shortages in sanctions-crippled Iraq. I assumed the pharmacist was a Christian (many are in the Arab world) and I tried to break the ice with him with some casual chatter about Rome, a city I've been fortunate enough to visit several times. Most Iraqi Christians, roughly 5 percent of the population, are Caldean Catholics and I assumed that the pharmacist's eyes would light up when I talked to him about Rome. The pharmacist told me he had an uncle in Milan and that his own son was a top-notch soccer player whose dream it was to play in the Italian *Seria A*. The pharmacist asked me if I could help his boy get a break. I wished him *buona fortuna*, but lamented that I knew nothing about the ball-kicking industry. I cautiously inquired more about his uncle in Milan, who turned out to be a priest.

After chatting for about ten minutes, I finally asked the pharmacist how his business was doing. It was my most probing question yet. It may be hard to imagine how nervous the Iraqi people were about talking to foreigners. Saddam Hussein's government treated almost all information like national secrets. A person's opinion, economic sentiments and loyalties were not to be expressed, especially in public and certainly not to foreigners. It was considered tantamount to treason. It was only safe for Iraqis to say that they were followers of the great leader Saddam Hussein and opponents of the United States government and Zionism. Anything more was wading into dangerous "political" discussions.

The pharmacist told me his business was fine. "Better than ever," he said.

"How can it be better than ever?" I pushed. "There's about to be a war."

"Maybe there will be a war, maybe there won't be. Hopefully there will not be a war."

The pharmacist's son, a boy of about sixteen, walked into the store and joined his father behind the sales counter. "Is this the soccer player?" I asked. I suggested that he write a letter to the European soccer federation, UEFA, and inquire about the procedures for trying out for a professional team. I had no idea if this strategy would work, but promised to bring him UEFA's address and mail the letter once I'd left Iraq. The pharmacist sold me a vitamin C powder, handed me my change and probably assumed he'd never see me again.

I returned to the hotel, copied down UEFA's mailing address from the Internet and drove back to the pharmacy after stopping in my room for some quality time on the commode.

I waited for all the customers to leave before I gave the pharmacist the address I'd found. The pharmacist then offered me tea, which we drank in a back room while his son manned the counter.

"Do you think there will be a war?" he asked, offering me a *Gauloises Blonds* cigarette.

"Yes, it's just a matter of time. I think it will be very soon," I said.

"It will be very difficult," he said.

"Do you want it?"

"Nobody wants war."

After pouring another glass of tea into my boiling stomach, I asked him what he was most worried about.

"It could get very ugly for Christians here. There are fundamentalists in Iraq who are capable of anything. They intimidate Christians," he said and went on to tell me that while he didn't like Saddam Hussein, whom he never mentioned by name despite our privacy, at least the Iraqi leader had a firm hand and controlled the fundamentalists. He told me stories about radical Sunni Muslim fanatics who put leaflets under the doors of Christian homes calling on them to convert and about bands of Muslim youths who would threaten and spit on Christian girls for not covering their hair with scarves like pious Muslim women. The pharmacist was frightened of what the Muslim fundamentalists would do during the chaos of the war, especially because Christian groups in the United States were supportive of military action, giving the impression in Iraq, he said, that all Christians were part of the war effort.

I told the pharmacist that my biggest concern was what would happen to foreigners once the war began. I told him that I was an American, which didn't seem to faze him at all. He told me that I could come to his store if I was ever in trouble and that he would hide me. He told me how to come to his house and said he'd shelter me there if he wasn't in the store.

"You know it would be very dangerous for you and your family if I were to be discovered with you?" I warned.

"It's not a problem," he said. He was a very generous and brave man. I found many Iraqis to be like him.

March 9

The journalists in Baghdad are spreading rumors like wildfire. No one really knows anything, or at least I don't think they do. Today is Sunday. The latest word among the pack is that the war could begin as early as Friday or a week from today. Everyone is trying to figure out what to do and where to go when the party starts.

Zafar was showing signs of stress. He sweated a lot, looked nervous and smoked constantly. Although the Iraqi media had the attitude "Impending war . . . what impending war?" the grapevine on the street was quietly humming with speculation. Zafar was starting to open up to me. I suspect he was trying to forge an alliance with a foreigner before the storm began. He was just as worried as I was.

"That's my house," Zafar said as we drove past a cluster of two-story unpainted concrete-and-brick buildings around a dirt courtyard, strewn with garbage, where children and stray dogs were playing.

"That's my son," he said of one of the children. Most people in the neighborhood were his relatives.

"Are you Sunni or Shiite Muslim?" I asked. Zafar flashed a devilish smile as if I'd just asked him a national secret that he was going to enjoy revealing.

While traditionally Baghdad has been a stronghold of Sunni Muslims (followers of "orthodox" Islam practiced in most of the Muslim world), many Shiite Muslims (predominant in the Middle East in Iran, Iraq and southern Lebanon) had steadily moved to the Iraqi capital from the countryside in search of work. About 60 percent of Iraq's 26 million people are Shiites, who tend to be poorer than the roughly 20 percent of Arab Sunnis who have dominated Iraq's political and economic elite. Saddam Hussein, for example, was a Sunni. The remainder of Iraq's population are Sunni Muslim Kurds, Christians, Turkomen and members of smaller ethnic and religious groups.

"I'm Shiite," Zafar said, "and I hate Saddam Hussein."

I was amazed. I'd never heard such a direct opinion in Iraq. "Saddam has killed so many Shiites, scared us and taken everything for himself and his bunch," Zafar said.

"What do you think will happen?" I asked.

"There is going to be fighting between Shiites and Sunnis. There will be killings in every house. People will take revenge on their neighbors. It will be a very big problem. That's the biggest danger."

"So you don't want the war?" I asked.

"Of course I want the war. I want it soon. If the Americans don't go ahead with the war, all Iraqis will cry tears of disappointment."

"Why do you want the war? To change the regime?" I asked.

"In Iraq we don't have anything. No money. No jobs. We've been cut off from the world's economy. Iraq is a rich country. We have so much oil and so many educated people. Iraq could be the richest country in the Middle East."

Zafar had already started fantasizing about how he would spend the windfall of money he expected would come immediately after the war ended. He told me the first thing he would buy would be a new car. He wanted a Toyota Super. Zafar also had his eye on an apartment where he could take his eighteen-year-old mistress, a university student whose parents had hired him to drive her to and from campus and gotten more than they'd paid for.

"Now, I can't even buy shoes," Zafar bemoaned. "This is the only pair I have," he said of the leather sandals he wore. He obviously expected me to buy him new shoes.

I'd been paying Zafar $30 a day. I suggested he spend some of it on a decent pair of shoes. Zafar's jowls dropped and his eyebrows leaped to his hairline. I decided it wasn't the appropriate time to quibble about money and promised to buy Zafar some new clothing. His face relaxed into its normal look of catlike self-satisfaction. We set off for a market in downtown Baghdad, where I also bought myself some local garb. The safari-style shirts and khaki pants I'd brought with me to Iraq made me obvious as a foreigner. If I needed to go underground, the new clothing would be helpful. I picked up a pair of dark blue cotton-polyester-blend pants, a gray shirt and black dress shoes. Most men in Baghdad wore Western-style clothing, mainly low-quality formal dress shirts, slacks and ill-fitting blazers in a variety of bright colors and synthetic materials. I also bought a bottle of black "Just For Men" hair dye.

After our shopping trip I promised Zafar that I'd treat him to the finest restaurant. He took me to a café specializing in grilled meat and fish. It felt like we were on a date. Effectively, I was courting his loyalty.

The restaurant was spacious and had a fountain in the middle made of stacked clay water jugs. It was crowded with Iraqi businessmen in dark suits and waiters in tuxedo shirts and ties. Zafar and I both ordered *kouzi*, an Iraqi specialty of boiled mutton served with rice topped with roasted almonds and raisins. Our table was covered in a sheet of transparent plastic for easy cleanup and on it was a plastic ashtray, a box of scented tissues for napkins and a bottle of a brown, locally made condiment with a label that said only, in English, SAUCE. There were hardly any luxury products in Iraq, and it was always a mystery to me how imported products ended up in the country. On the packet of Marlboros Zafar smoked, for example, was printed: CHINA DUTY FREE. One can only imagine the astonishing journey the cigarettes must have had. One journalist had described to me how she'd gone for a massage at the Al-Rashid Hotel and that the masseuse, having no moisturizing cream, had sprayed her back with window cleaner.

In the car after lunch I told Zafar that I wanted him to help me hire a policeman. Since I didn't have the correct visa, I thought having someone with police credentials on my payroll would be useful. I hoped he'd be able to get me through roadblocks (there weren't any roadblocks in Baghdad yet, but I assumed that once the war started they'd be set up on every corner) or at least be able to convince other policemen or Baath party officials to release me if I was detained. I told Zafar that I needed someone who understood the risk, knew how to use a gun if necessary and who was obviously not a Saddam loyalist. Zafar said he had a friend from his neighborhood he thought might fit the bill.

Back at the Flowers Land, I flipped on local television, hoping to find some clues about the start date for the war. The broadcasts, however, were filled with Iraqi music videos with singers lionizing Saddam Hussein and video sequences highlighting Iraq's natural and archeological wonders. The newsreader led the nightly news bulletin with, "Today, Zionist forces arrested twelve Palestinians in the West Bank." It was so off the mark. Such a relatively common event wouldn't have led the newscast even in the Palestinian territories, let alone in Iraq on the brink of a devastating war. The report was followed by a story about an exhibition organized by the Iraqi oil ministry to commemorate the numerous official visits Saddam Hussein had paid to the oil ministry headquarters. "These poor people, having to listen to this nonsense for their entire lives. It must be mind-numbing," I thought. The news broadcast ended with a quote from Saddam Hussein, read by the announcer with great reverence. It translated to "Iraq is the great tree of life of Iraq." I still have no idea what it meant.

The broadcast was typical of the Iraqi media, which portrayed Saddam to be a godlike incarnation of a military hero, a heavenly prophet and a sage all wrapped into one bundle of joy with a mustache. When Iraqi officials said Saddam Hussein's name in Arabic they always followed it with "May God keep and protect him."

The first time I was in Iraq I was astonished at the depth of Saddam's cult of personality. During the October 2002 referendum, Saddam's long-serving right-hand man, Ezzat Ibrahim, told reporters that 100 percent of Iraqis had reelected Saddam on the "Day of Allegiance" (the Iraqi title of the referendum) just as Muslims had chosen to follow the Prophet Mohammed during the early days of Islam. In other Muslim societies I'd seen, comparing oneself to Mohammed was so blasphemous it would have invoked a *fatwa*, or Islamic ruling, demanding execution. Winning by a ridiculous majority was fairly common in the Middle East. Both Egypt's President Mubarak and his Tunisian counterpart have won referendums with officially more than 98 percent of the popular vote. But 100 percent was a result that must have made even North Korea's Kim Jong Il jealous.

I switched off the television and headed to the businessmen center to have a drink of whiskey with Mohammed the computer hacker.

March 10

No more drinking! I'm angry with myself! I'd been with Mohammed and a man who said he was a Lebanese businessman. We were having a good time, drinking and

talking in the business center. I let my guard down because
of the whiskey. We were talking about the war. I introduced
the subject! How stupid of me! I should have kept my
mouth shut!

I woke up that morning and wanted to hide in my room. I
knew I'd gone too far, talking about the war in the current cli-
mate. It had just slipped out. Now I was worried I'd made
myself suspect, especially because the Lebanese businessman
I'd been talking to with Mohammed had started picking out
inconsistencies in my story. I'd been telling people I lived in
Egypt, for example, instead of Jerusalem.

"I thought you lived in Egypt, but now you are speaking
like a Palestinian," I remembered the Lebanese man telling
me. "Have you ever been to Israel?"

I swallowed hard. After a few drinks I'd drifted into a
Palestinian accent. I'd spent so much time with Palestinians
over the past three years that their accent was freshest in my
mind.

"No, I've never been there," I said. "I must have picked up
something of a Palestinian accent by watching television. You
know most of the correspondents on al-Jazeera are Lebanese
or Palestinian. I watch a lot of television."

The Lebanese guy didn't seem to buy it. He was too smart.
He started quizzing me about Hezbollah and Israeli weapons
and seemed to know what he was talking about. He was probing me to see what I knew.

Later that morning, Zafar pulled me aside in the lobby and told me Mohammed had been chatting with him in private. Mohammed had evidently told him that I'd asked if he wanted Saddam Hussein to be removed. As soon as Zafar mentioned it, I remembered the conversation. I was furious with myself. Now I wasn't sure if Mohammed was going to report me. Why else would he be telling Zafar what I'd said?

"Don't worry, I'm very good at keeping secrets," Zafar told me. "You should pay me because I'm so good at keeping secrets," implying that he could easily stop being good at keeping secrets. I could have killed him.

I saw Mohammed a short while later and didn't bring up my talk with Zafar. I pretended that nothing had happened.

"Why don't you have a press badge yet?" Mohammed asked me. Nearly all the other reporters at this stage were wearing laminated credentials issued by the press center. I didn't have one because of my human shield status. "I know it's because you're a spy," Mohammed added. It seemed by the tone of his voice as if he was joking, but it was hardly the time or place. I was worried about his comment because in many ways I did look suspicious. I was a young American man. I had improper paperwork. I was an Arabic speaker. I'd spent time in Israel. And I had a room full of illegal equipment I couldn't account for and $20,000 in cash wrapped around my ankle.

I certainly didn't need the attention Mohammed was drawing to me; attention I'd stupidly drawn to myself! I decided to visit the Al-Rashid to see how other Western reporters were reading the situation.

All the reporters I met at the Al-Rashid were cagey and vague about their plans. Although it was frustrating, it was understandable. Everyone in Baghdad was trying to be strategic, including me. People were only telling half-truths, if not out and out lies, to each other. No one was completely sharing information. The journalists would test each other with questions but try not to reveal anything. I found it rather distressing. While I was at the Al-Rashid I was approached by many other correspondents who knew I spoke Arabic. They tried to glean bits of information from me while offering none in return. I told people that I was most worried about the behavior of the local officials, but that I had my own problems because of my visa status. Some journalists seemed to take special pleasure in the fact that my visa status was so shaky. I guess it made them feel better knowing that they were in a somewhat stronger position than I was. I remember distinctly hoping the environment would ameliorate once the war began. I feared, however, that the prevailing mood of backstabbing competitiveness would only worsen as the pressure mounted. I wondered how I would have reacted if a colleague needed my help in a crisis during the war. Would I refuse to save myself or protect my delicate footing? I didn't know the answer, but hoped I would be brave, unselfish and get away with it.

I hated going to the Al-Rashid Hotel. The place was swarming with intelligence officers and nosey drivers. Everything I'd done that day drew attention. I needed to get a minder from the press center, a reporting badge, a government-recognized driver and start playing by the rules or I was going to get burned. When I left the Al-Rashid, I felt more alone than I ever had in my life.

On the way back to the Flowers Land, Zafar told me he'd found a policeman. He was a major in the traffic department and hated the government. There was only one problem with him, Zafar said nonchalantly: He was an alcoholic.

March 11

> I'm going to the press center today to try to sort out the visa myself. I'm of two minds: If I can manage to register myself properly, I'll stay in Iraq and cover the war. If I cannot, I will make an honorable exit as soon as possible.

I went to the press center, breezed by the front office and walked into the room where they printed the badges. I introduced myself to a local official, gave him the $10 processing fee and two photographs. The place was buzzing with activity. The official took one of my passport photos, stapled it to a badge, wrote my name on it and handed it back to me without looking up from his desk. I was set! I hung the ID on a string around my neck like a badge of honor and left the room floating on air. But as I was leaving the press center I passed the director's office next to the main exit. The manager wanted to

know who I was and how I'd gotten the badge. After I failed
to convince him, he took the badge and told me I was not
allowed to do any reporting. He said I would have to leave
Iraq in the next three days. I was completely crestfallen.

Before coming to Iraq, I'd assumed that once the war
began—which I imagined would be sudden and terrifying—
the visa system, if not the entire Iraqi government, would collapse. But the onset of the war was proving to be progressing
much more slowly than I'd anticipated. With each passing
day the psychological tension was mounting and the press
center was growing stricter. No official wanted to be the first
to break the rules. The government bureaucrats, who had
years of training at stamping papers, were especially mindful
to do their jobs by the letter. Faced with a crisis, they'd
reverted to doing what they knew best: following the rules. I
was starting to accept the fact that I wouldn't be able to cover
the war in Iraq.

March 14

Today is my last day. The mood here is frighteningly
tense. All of the journalists are seriously debating what to do.
Everyone is so secretive. Some reporters have started to leave
the country. This buildup to war has been murder on our
nerves. I don't want to be here with the wrong paperwork.

I did, however, see one ray of hope. I'd heard from contacts in Jordan that Iraqi officials at the embassy in Amman

were now issuing reporting visas. Evidently, they'd discovered that many reporters in Baghdad were leaving the country and wanted to have some coverage. At that moment I decided that I was willing to stay and report on the war if I could only get my hands on a proper visa. I couldn't take my equipment out of the country because I didn't have any customs forms for it, so I left the $20,000, satellite phone, flak jacket and all of my clothing in my hotel room at the Flowers Land, jumped into a GMC Suburban with a few hundred dollars in my pocket and set off for Amman. I knew there was a very real possibility I wouldn't be returning to Iraq anytime soon.

March 16

I'm back in Baghdad and finally in business! I drove to
Jordan and back over the last 36 hours. I slept the night in the
GMC. I was issued a journalist visa on the spot!

As I left Amman it finally hit me what I was really getting into. Until this point, I'd mainly been worrying about my visa status. Now I saw the real problem. As I headed toward the Iraqi border I seriously considered telling the Jordanian driver to turn around and head back to Amman. I still didn't have a commitment from ABC News, and as Amman receded in the distance, I also wondered if I was being irresponsible and selfish by going back to Baghdad. "At least I don't have any kids," I thought. I also knew how depressed I'd be if I gave up and drove back to Amman.

I asked the driver to wait a minute before he crossed to the Iraqi side of the border checkpoint. I felt like I was on the banks of the River Styx, looking into the underworld. I took several deep breaths to settle the adrenaline coursing in my veins and told the driver to go ahead. I was committed.

The driver again picked up an Iraqi intelligence officer at the border, and, again, I had to pretend to be asleep and not speak Arabic. The pillow I rested my head on in the backseat stank of gasoline. The driver smoked constantly and played a cassette recording of the Koran for most of the drive. I found it easier to sleep to than Jennifer Lopez.

When I arrived in Baghdad I was extremely focused. I went to the Al-Rashid Hotel to see what had happened to the other journalists in town, but most of them had either left the country or were packing up to leave.

Like the other major networks, the ABC team was closing its operation. The chief producer in town told me, however, that the New York editors had reached a deal with a British newspaper reporter to cover Baghdad during the war. The ABC team had given her some reporting equipment and packed up the rest.

I drove to the Flowers Land Hotel, furious. I felt I'd been shut out just when I was ready. I called a friend at CBS to see if they were interested in using me. I wanted to call NBC, too, but I didn't have their telephone number. ABC did eventually offer me a retainer and said I would split the reporting duties with the British newspaper reporter. The editors stressed that I could leave Baghdad anytime I felt unsafe and that I would be paid regardless of whether I stayed or not. I thought it was a very professional way of taking money out of the decision-making process.

I rushed back to the Al-Rashid to see if I could grab any equipment from the ABC team before it pushed off. I took an extra satellite phone, some cash, an extra chemical/biological suit, a gas mask and a few extension cords that didn't plug into anything.

Back at the Flowers Land, Zafar seemed happy to see me. I hadn't told him or anyone else that I'd left for Jordan—I'd just disappeared. Of course, Zafar wanted money from me. He told me an official from the intelligence service based at the al-Rashid had approached him while I was away and demanded to know who I was and what I'd been paying. Zafar explained that I was a reporter and that I paid him $10 a day. The intelligence officer reprimanded Zafar, arguing that $10 was too little. Zafar said he'd been instructed to charge me $100 a day and to hand over half of it to the intelligence officer. Zafar said he'd also been instructed to write daily reports about me. He promised to write lies.

"Don't do that," I said, not knowing if Zafar had any idea how to lie. "I'm not going to any prohibited sites. Just tell them where we go," I said. "That's better."

I was actually somewhat pleased to hear about the intelligence service's minor extortion ring. It seemed to indicate that the intelligence agents were petty and greedy rather than loyal to Saddam and his ideology. If their main concern was extracting $50 a day from me I figured I might just be all right.

March 17

The mood in Baghdad has suddenly changed. It is as if the Iraqis are finally starting to realize that this war is really coming. There is now heavy traffic, almost all of it heading out of town. I've seen shop owners boarding up their businesses. Jewelers and watchmakers are clearing out their windows and display cases. I watch people put packaging tape over their shop windows. There is now clearly tension in the air. It's as if people were sleeping, but are now awake. It seems that the decision by the United States and Britain not to push for a new UN resolution has convinced people that the fighting will truly happen.

There had been about 700 journalists in Baghdad at the beginning of March. Now there were only about 150, almost all of them Europeans.

At the press center I met another official named Kazem, Uday al-Ta'e's deputy. I had a good feeling about him. There was no hate in his eyes, nor the dead stare some Iraqi bureaucrats had, like that of prisoners on death row who'd lost hope. Kazem seemed earnest in his desire to run a well-organized press center. I took a risk with him and spoke Arabic. Most of the time, I'd been conversing in purposely broken Arabic. They already knew I spoke some of the language, but I wanted to keep them guessing how much. It was harder for the Iraqi government to control journalists who spoke Arabic. Most of the minders also served as translators for reporters and I'd seen them filter information during interviews. Kazem, however, seemed genuinely pleased that I'd spent the time to learn the language.

"Why are you staying when everyone else is leaving?" he asked me. I think he really wanted to know.

I said there must be some journalists who are as *samid* as the Iraqi people. He laughed out loud and put his arm over my shoulder. *Samid* means both steadfast and brave, and is the favorite adjective Iraqis use to describe themselves. I'd heard it in many of the nationalist songs played on Iraqi radio and television, and it's also often used in Arab media to describe the Palestinians. It is the ultimate shame among Arabs to be called a coward; it is the highest honor to be *samid*.

Armed with my new badge, I met my minder, Abu Sattar. I could tell instantly he was going to be a problem. He had jet-black hair, a stocky build, a square face and a thick mustache. He looked remarkably like Saddam Hussein. After discussing the political situation with him for a few minutes, I concluded that Abu Sattar was either a complete fool, totally brainwashed, or thought that I was daft. He pretended that nothing was out of the ordinary.

I asked him about the people I'd seen fleeing Baghdad. He pretended he didn't know what I was talking about. It was just bad traffic, he told me. I could tell he was not going to let me roam freely and report. He was to be avoided.

During this period I also met Ali, the nineteen-year-old who would soon become my trusted driver and friend—the only person in whom I had complete faith during the war. Ali—who'd worked for other American networks that left Baghdad—was skinny, quiet, sensitive and very shy. He had a delicate face and long eyelashes, but despite his timid appearance he would prove to be incredibly brave and loyal. Ali didn't smoke, curse or drive recklessly. He was polite and deferential. Ali's car, a white Toyota Super—the vehicle that Zafar wanted to buy—was clean and appeared to be well maintained. He had a spare tire, for example, and the tools to fix it, unlike Zafar, who'd asked me to supply him with both.

Zafar was waiting for me on the couch in the hotel lobby like a spider when I pulled up in Ali's car. I told Zafar that I didn't want to use him anymore, but would continue to pay him. I wanted him to be close by in case I needed him.

I asked Zafar if he'd taken any precautions for his family now that the war was approaching. I wasn't surprised to hear that he hadn't. After buying Zafar several cartons of canned food, bottled water and a shortwave radio so he and his family could listen to the news, I told Zafar that I wanted him to find me more drivers and a safe house outside of town. I asked him if there were any developments regarding his policeman friend, and stressed that in a crisis, I'd need to be able to find both of them at a moment's notice. The best way to do that, I thought, was to lodge both Zafar and the policeman in a hotel room. I booked them a two-bedroom apartment downtown in Zafar's name and paid for a week in advance. I refused to buy them whiskey despite Zafar's pleading. I didn't want the policeman smashed when I needed him.

I called ABC's foreign desk and learned President Bush was making a speech that night. The editors thought he might be announcing the start of the war. The desk editors also told me that the British newspaper reporter had left Baghdad, so I was alone.

I jumped in a local taxi and headed to the press center, where Ismail was operating a live satellite uplink camera ABC was leasing from Ismail's company, IHA. As I rode over, I wondered what President Bush might say in the impending speech. Would he announce that fighters were already in the air, headed for Iraq? I thought about an e-mail I'd received from my mother earlier that day.

Richard . . .

In light of developments during the last few hours it seems perfectly clear that you should be leaving immediately! We, your family, urge you not to delay. Chaos and panic can develop in an instant, and you don't want to miss the last bus out! Always leave yourself with a comfortable margin, and in this case make it extra comfortable. We love you, and I am worried sick!

Mom

It was her second e-mail in as many days.

> *Richard the time has come to leave, please. To hell with the*
> *networks, just get going and head out!!! I love you.*
>
> *Mom*

President Bush's speech didn't make me feel much better either.

> *. . . All the decades of deceit and cruelty have now reached*
> *an end. Saddam Hussein and his sons must leave Iraq within*
> *forty-eight hours. Their refusal to do so will result in military*
> *conflict, commenced at a time of our choosing. For their own*
> *safety, all foreign nationals—including journalists and*
> *inspectors—should leave Iraq immediately. . . .*

The president's call for journalists to leave Iraq sent chills down my back and made my legs shake as I stood listening to it through my earpiece on a balcony above the press center.

CHAPTER FOUR

THE CURRENCY EXCHANGE TRADER was practically in tears. "There's no market! There's no market!" he was yelling as I slipped into his store on Saadoon Street. The forty-eight-hour deadline was destroying his business. Ali was waiting in his car outside, so I was blissfully alone. It was rare to be able to wander around Baghdad. But Abu Sattar at least was lazy and sloppy, making it easy to avoid him, which is what I was doing at the currency exchange store.

I'd asked Ali to pull over while we were on the way to the press center to pick up Abu Sattar. I wanted to get an idea of what was happening in the city without the company of my personal spy. I wasn't filming inside the currency exchange bureau—a small office illuminated by a single fluorescent tube and furnished with a chest-high bill counter and a scale—but only listening. On the wall behind the countertop was one of the posters of Saddam Hussein that all shopkeepers were obligated to display. This one showed Saddam in his youth, when he'd been a rather handsome man with a well-trimmed mustache, clear eyes and a perfect coif of black hair.

Saadoon Street was—and remains—a main thoroughfare in central Baghdad lined with jewelers, camera shops and movie theaters displaying hand-painted posters of Hollywood flops, including *Barb Wire*, starring Pamela Anderson, and B movies with racy titles. One B flick, entitled *Lazy Girl*, had a poster showing a bewhiskered simpering old geezer whose face was sandwiched between the rear ends of two plucky young vixens in hot pants. Saadoon Street was Baghdad's equivalent to New York's Times Square before its revival in the 1990s: Baghdad's seedy underbelly. But unlike in New York, Pamela Anderson in patent leather (her cleavage barely painted over in black ink, in a nod—or perhaps a wink—to Muslim sensitivities) was as piquant as Baghdad got, at least in public. Behind closed doors Baghdad had its share of brothels, speakeasies and ultra-private clubs for Saddam's *familiari* and potentates.

"There's no market!" the currency trader kept crying to his friend, who shook his head in sympathy.

Both men seemed oblivious to my presence. The shop owner threw down a bundle of Iraqi dinars on his counter in disgust and banged his hand in frustration against the scale— an old-fashioned model with two arms that he balanced with cylindrical weights made of brass. Since the 1991 Gulf War, inflation in Iraq had been rampant. By 2003, many currency traders found it easier to weigh bundles of money than count through reams of bills. A thousand dollars, for example, was about ten thousand separate 250-dinar notes, the most common denomination in Iraq. The currency trader in front of me lamented to his friend that he had a back room full of dinars that evidently nobody wanted to buy after President Bush imposed the deadline. The trader feared his cache of cash would soon be little more than souvenirs.

I exchanged a hundred dollars. The trader practically threw 300,000 dinars at me. The dinar had slipped 30 percent against the dollar overnight. He made me feel like I was stealing from him as he tossed me a black plastic bag filled with twelve hundred notes. It was about as heavy as two weekday newspapers.

The currency trader wasn't the only person now feeling war's dank breath. Vendors emerged from nowhere, like umbrella hawkers in New York when it rains, and started selling plastic jerricans on street corners. Iraqis were lining up to buy the plastic jugs to stockpile water and gasoline. Iraqis who had lived through both the Iran-Iraq War (1980–1988) and the 1991 Gulf War knew about shortages. I also saw Iraqi workmen loading a truck in front of the Interior Ministry with files, computers and office furniture. The government evidently believed the building would be on the US's target list. The Interior Ministry kept files on criminals (both ordinary and political) as well as more mundane, but important, documents such as marriage certificates and land deeds. "What will happen if all this is destroyed?" I wondered. "It'll be chaos and keep lawyers in business for decades trying to sort it out."

But the biggest change I noticed after President Bush put Iraq on two days' notice was the emergence of the Baath party on the streets of Baghdad. The Baath party—whose presence had always been felt in Iraq but seldom seen on the streets— had suddenly descended on the city. Officially known as the Baath Arab Socialist party, the group was the only recognized political organization in Iraq. Members of unauthorized parties, such as the Shiite Daawa party, were arrested, executed and dumped in mass graves. Membership in Saddam's Baath party was mandatory for all Iraqis in positions of leadership and power, no matter how petty. Any factory foreman, government administrator or school principal, for example, was sure to be a Baath party member. The Baath party also had armed divisions. After President Bush's speech, it became obvious that these armed units had been deputized as guardians of Baghdad. I was somewhat surprised to see them setting up checkpoints and guard posts on street corners. I'd expected Republican Guards, who were better-armed and better-trained professional soldiers, to be given the task. I wouldn't find out until later what had happened to the Republican Guards, and of their treason.

As I drove to the press center to collect Abu Sattar, I watched hundreds of Baath party militiamen piling sandbags into small, circular guard posts. A pair of loyalists armed with Kalashnikovs manned each of the makeshift turrets. The posts were being put up at every major intersection and in front of all main government buildings. Over the next few days, I would see thousands of armed Baath party members take to the streets. It was quite a show of force. At the time I was convinced that Baghdad would become a slaughterhouse if US troops tried to storm the city, which was why I was so frantically setting up safe houses and equipping them with food, water, crowbars and generators. I'd set up two others in small hotels near the Flowers Land just in case.

"When the fighting starts, most of these people will stay at home," Ali said as we drove past a guard post. I was surprised. It was unusual for Ali to speak when not directly asked a question. "They won't fight," he added without taking his eyes off the road. Ali didn't want to make it too obvious that he was talking to me, or about the Baath members. This was a standard procedure in Baghdad, a city without trust. It is not an exaggeration to say that everyone in Baghdad did everything—even innocuous things like shopping—as secretly as possible. Iraqis were afraid of their neighbors and even, sometimes, family members. I doubt Ali even realized how secretive he was—it had become second nature to him. Ali had never lived a single day in a free society. Unlike Zafar, who I suspect told me "secrets" like his alleged hatred of Saddam so I would continue to buy him goodies, I think Ali told me what he believed out of a combination of loyalty, friendship, honesty and, most of all, naiveté. Ali didn't seem to know how to lie, although he seldom spoke the whole truth. When a traffic cop leaned into our car window one day and asked Ali who I was and where we were headed, Ali passed me off as a foreign peace activist from Egypt who'd come to Iraq to express support for the regime. I'd never asked him to misrepresent me. He just didn't feel like telling the policeman the truth. In Iraq, the truth never helped. Fiction—as long as it was what the state wanted to hear—was more accepted, no matter how implausible. "They don't need to know who you are," Ali told me.

With me, however, Ali was honest to the point of making me embarrassed. He refused to take money for running errands and brought me change for everything he bought. He told me exactly where he was at all times and there were never any inconsistencies. I trusted Ali's word 100 percent, and yet watched him be flexible with the truth every day. In Iraq, truth was relative and seldom helpful.

Ali often acted with the starry-eyed innocence of a small-town kid who'd never seen a big city. Even though there were almost five million people living in Baghdad, the city was in many ways more isolated than a Midwestern American town. I told Ali that I'd driven three thousand miles from New York to California without once being stopped or questioned by government authorities. He couldn't believe such a place existed. Ali behaved like a boy who lived in a small world, which—tragically—was the dark infernal world created by Saddam Hussein. I asked Ali what he thought about Saddam Hussein. His answer was typically both innocent and evasive. "Please don't ask me that," he said. His opinion was diamond clear. Zafar would have grinned at me with his black teeth, revealed a little snippet of his opinion and implied that if I bought him a present he'd tell me more. Ali didn't engage in this truth strip tease.

Ali would later prove to be right about the Baath party militiamen. During Saddam Hussein's nearly three decades in power, the Iraqi dictator had greatly expanded and popularized the party, bringing what had once been an elite Pan-Arab political association to millions of poor Iraqis. Most of the Baath "fighters" I saw on the streets had day jobs at places like the post office. Many of them were over fifty years old. Baath party guards were somewhat comparable to American volunteer firemen—tough, patriotic working-class men. They were not trained killers or terrorists, nor were they highly paid or motivated. They were nothing like the *fedayeen*—the band of thugs, fanatics and criminals led by Saddam's cruel son Uday.

There was one key difference between the guards and American volunteer firemen, however. The Baath party members had the backing of a dictator, which gave them power to abuse. Members intimidated nonmembers, informed on them and would sometimes extort bribes from people without political connections. There were also patently sinister divisions of Baath militiamen, whom I saw driving through Baghdad in pickup trucks with machine guns mounted on tripods. These pickups were combing through poor neighborhoods, breaking up congregations of people. They traveled house to house and took roll call in an effort to prevent an internal revolt now that President Bush had thrown down the gauntlet.

When I finally rolled up to the press center I found Abu

Sattar stamping his foot like a date who'd been left waiting on the street corner.

"Why are you late?" he snapped.

"I overslept," I said and gushed apologies. "Can you please take me on a tour of the city? I haven't seen anything yet," I begged Abu Sattar. My goal was to make Abu Sattar feel like he'd done something and let him write whatever report he needed to file on me, so that he'd feel satisfied and I could get on with my business.

We drove around for an hour.

"You see everything is very normal. Just look," he told me.

I looked at people boxing up stores and putting tape over windows. There was a steady stream of cars heading out of the city.

"Abu Sattar, how can you say everything is normal? Look at what people are doing," I insisted. "People are closing stores and heading out of town."

"No, everyone is staying. I am here and my children went to school today."

"Then why is everyone driving out of the city?"

"They aren't."

After we'd been driving around for another half hour, I told Abu Sattar that I wasn't feeling well and thanked him profusely. I dropped him off at the press center.

"I'm going to get some more sleep back at the hotel," I told him.

"You are very lazy. The other journalists are all working on their reports," he told me.

"Just don't tell my bosses," I joked and gave him a playful slap on the back before setting off to see more Iraqis by myself. It was a silly game, but I had to pretend not to be ignoring Abu Sattar.

As we parted, Abu Sattar told me that the press center had ordered all journalists to move out of wherever we were staying and into either the Palestine, the Al-Rashid or the al-Mansour, another of Baghdad's major state-run hotels.

My choice of the Palestine was relatively easy. It was tall, providing a clear view of the city, and it was across the Tigris River from the main part of Baghdad where the press center and other government buildings and presidential palaces were located. While the Al-Rashid and al-Mansour were more solidly built than the Palestine—which seemed like it was made of papier-mâché and would sway whenever the bombs fell—they were both flanked by government buildings. The Pentagon had also been leaking reports to journalists that the Al-Rashid in particular was on the military's target list. The Al-Rashid was rumored to have a network of tunnels beneath it and to be a communication center for the Iraqi security forces.

I rushed to the Palestine to try to secure a room.

Only the jugglers were missing from the frantic circus of activity I found at the Palestine by the time I got there. All of the journalists still in town (now about a hundred) were begging for rooms and trying to sneak in illegal equipment, including satellite phones, electric generators and gasoline, without the hotel manager, or any meddling press center minders, noticing. Technically, sat phones had to be stored at the press center, although no one did that, instead paying $50 for the official in charge to look the other way. And the manager of the Palestine didn't want people bringing tanks of gasoline to their rooms, which was certainly understandable. I managed to book three rooms at the Palestine on different sides of the building. I wanted to have as many perspectives of the city as possible. I was also pleased to discover that for a five-dollar tip, a porter named Ahmed (whom I would continue to tip five to ten dollars a day for the next month) put all of my equipment into a dirty cardboard box, which he brought to my room on the fourteenth floor in the service elevator, gas tank and generator included. By the end of the day, the Palestine Hotel was explosive with all the gasoline inside of it.

But there was a bigger problem with the Palestine. It was full of men dying to become suicide bombers. There were about twenty-five of them. Most were Arabs between twenty and thirty years old with scraggly beards. There were also several Asians, including one man who looked to be in his early twenties. He had unkempt hair and wore a green bandana around his forehead that said, in Arabic, THERE IS NO GOD BUT GOD, AND MOHAMMED IS THE PROPHET OF GOD, the Islamic proclamation of faith. They were officially called Muslim human shields, but many of the reporters—including me—suspected they were really human bombs. A Greek journalist, Efi Pentaraki, who was in the room next to mine on the fourteenth floor, said she recognized several of the Arab volunteers from a training camp for suicide bombers she'd visited two weeks earlier. The base, run by the Iraqi government, was also filmed by al-Jazeera. A few days after arriving at the Palestine, I struck up a conversation with one of the "Muslim human shields" from Tunisia. We were in the elevator together, and he told me point-blank that he'd come to Iraq to fight the Americans and be a martyr for Islam. I wished him well and got off on the next floor, not wanting this particular individual to know which room I was staying in. I wondered if the wannabe martyrs (who were guests of the Iraqi government) had explosives in the hotel, or if they intended to take Westerners hostage. There was also some talk among reporters that the Muslim volunteers were members of al-Qaeda, but it was impossible to know.

That night, I headed over to the Flowers Land and saw Mohammed the hacker sitting in the lobby, pale and sweating. He looked as if he'd been awake for thirty-six hours. He gave me an affectionate hug and we went up to my room and talked for about two hours.

"Richard, you know why I like computers so much? It's because I trust them more than people," he said, puffing heavily on a cigarette. "Focusing on computers makes me forget the world around me, the wars, the government, the rumors of what might happen.

"I was nine years old when the 1991 attack began. I'd been sleeping, and when I woke up my father told me it was a military training exercise. I remember the sky was full of fire from the air defenses. It was red. Then my father told me that the

United States had started attacking us. I clung to my father and slept in his bed and cried and didn't sleep. Then my father told me, 'Don't worry, it will only be for one day. They want to destroy some things and it will be over.' My sister, who was thirteen years at the time, slept for the whole night. She never even woke up.

"Before the war, my family was rich. We changed the car every month. My father was an engineer with a German construction company. I had everything I wanted: chocolates, Snickers, Twix, Mars . . . whole boxes of them. But during the war, we were forced to make bread. My mother had never made bread before. She was also an engineer like my father. What she baked was like a solid rock. We had no power either. No one had expected this war could happen after the war with Iran. When the power was cut, all of the food in the fridge went bad. We hadn't been prepared. My mother was crying like mad. My brother was on the front lines in the army.

"At nine, I saw real life," Mohammed went on, pouring out everything he'd been holding inside. There really was a feeling that the apocalypse was coming. "Most people will never know how hard life is until they are at least twenty," he said, "but at nine, I couldn't play, watch TV, or drink water. We broke pipes in the floor of our house and drank the water that had been sitting inside of them for two days. It was really dirty. It tasted like you were drinking a puddle in the street that a thousand frogs had been playing in.

"Before the war I thought life was easy. I don't want to

make you cry, Richard, I just want to give you an impression of how I was living. It established the way I think and see the world."

"I think you should try to get out of town if you can," I told him. "It's going to get ugly here."

Mohammed agreed, but said he didn't want to leave his grandparents, who refused to leave their home.

"Mohammed, I have several rooms at the Palestine Hotel. If the situation escalates, you're welcome to stay in one of them. You can pack in as many people as you can," I said. Mohammed offered to shelter me at his home, or at a friend's house. "I'll pick you up no matter where you are and hide you," he said. I thanked him and headed back to the Palestine. Eight hours later, the bombings began.

War, Day One (March 20, 03, 5:30 A.M. Baghdad time)

Cruise missiles struck. Forty or so of them. The US says it tried to hit a "target of opportunity," i.e., Saddam. It happened at 5:30 A.M. I'd been bracing for it, even though Pentagon sources said the war wouldn't begin until Friday (March 21). I'd expected more . . . more sound, more anti-aircraft fire. I could also hear jets overhead, but I couldn't see them. Saddam went on the radio four hours later with a message describing how the attacks had begun at the time of the morning prayers, which they did. It seems he survived. The speech was definitely written after the attack.

I'd expected Armageddon, fireballs raining from the sky, the earth shaking like it had been hammered by an angry god. Instead, the first night was something of a dud. I did hear the crackling of anti-aircraft fire, which exploded in the sky like red fireworks, and many thundering booms in the city and flashes of light. But compared to what I'd been prepared for, it was almost anti-climactic.

The Pentagon later announced that the first night had been a hastily organized attempt on Saddam Hussein's life. The attack would kick off a debate (more among the US media than Iraqis I met) about Saddam's fate and health, which would last for the rest of the war.

The first speech Saddam gave after the cruise missile barrage encapsulated Iraq's spin on the war. He began by telling Iraqis that "the day of great Jihad" had arrived. The message that Iraq was fighting a Jihad—a war in which Muslims are duty bound to defend Islamic lands from non-Muslim invaders—was ubiquitous in Iraqi propaganda.

"The aggressors," the speech continued, "want to usurp Iraq's freedom and strip Iraqis of their pride." He went on to accuse the US and British forces of having "evil imperialist and Zionist intentions." The call on Iraqis to defend their dignity, and the nebulous link with Israel, were also pervasive throughout the war.

"Do not be frightened," Saddam said. "I promise you that we will resist!

"Long live Iraq and long live Palestine! Long live those

who love peace and security! This is a war against all Arabs and all Muslims. Iraq will be the enemy's graveyard, with God's assistance!"

I met Ali in the lobby of the Palestine on the war's first "morning after" before heading over to the press center. I didn't quite know what to expect as I left the hotel and waded out into what was now an enemy capital at war. I felt totally alone, and vulnerable. While I'd never thought there was anyone who would swoop in and rescue me, now I understood exactly how on my own I really was, without a country, an embassy or friendly police in a city under attack by my own government. I wondered how much of Baghdad had been damaged by the bombs we'd dropped on the city, and what would happen if I ran into an angry mob. I pictured people venting frustrations on me as an American—lynching me—and I could even sympathize with their actions.

The Information Ministry building was a beehive of activity, and for the first time, there were armed guards standing by the doors. Despite this, I was shocked at how normal everything seemed. The mood wasn't panicked or enraged, just slightly more chaotic than usual. I searched for Abu Sattar but couldn't find him. I poked around the ministry's offices until I saw buses pulling away from in front of the press center. An Iraqi selling tiny cups of sweet tea and wafer cookies told me the buses were taking reporters on a tour to visit bombed sites. I was constantly finding out information this way. Press conferences and government events always seemed to be organized in the last minute. After flagging down the bus, I joined the tour, which only stopped at a hospital and an oil refinery, where reporters were introduced to a group of my erstwhile colleagues, foreign human shields.

Back at the press center, I was told that Abu Sattar had left Baghdad for "family business." "Coward," I thought. I never saw him again. He was probably hiding, waiting for the war to be over, which he assumed would be soon. I did, too, and I think everyone in Baghdad did at first. Abu Sattar, like so many others I'd later learn, had been a mere functionary who wasn't loyal to Saddam Hussein. He'd fled as I'd anticipated the entire regime would if the war had been as devastating and sudden as the Pentagon had promised, dropping the Mother of All Bombs and other weapons that were similarly advanced. I'd expected American troops to parachute into Baghdad within days of an initial, spectacular, camera-friendly, incinerating air assault.

Instead, I was profoundly disappointed to learn that US and British forces had chosen to fight their way to Baghdad from southern Iraq—the hardest possible route. If the entire war had been staged from eastern Jordan, for example, the US Army could simply have rolled into Baghdad along a paved highway and been in the city in a single day. Instead, the US and British forces trudged up from Kuwait, making me chew my fingernails as they did.

I was assigned a new minder, who replaced Abu Sattar. He

was a tall man of about sixty-five, with long fingers, a long neck and a brown corduroy suit that he wore every day. His name was Abu Annas and he had a dignified air about him. He stood upright and spoke clearly and politely. He had the personality and appearance of a tired middle-school science teacher who always followed the rules. Unlike Abu Sattar, however, Abu Annas proved to be brave and would stay with me until the final days of the war.

On the first day, Abu Annas took me to what would become daily press briefings by the now famous Iraqi information minister, Mohammed Saeed al-Sahaf. Al-Sahaf and the interior minister were standing behind a podium in a small, modern building near the press center. The interior minister promised that the Americans would find "Iraq fighters in every home, behind every rock, tree and wall!" He was also brandishing a silver-plated Kalashnikov the likes of which Al Capone would have envied. Al-Sahaf was a short, bespectacled, acerbic man with a violent temper, a booming yet nasal voice and an extremely low boiling point. He had once been a local Baath party enforcer, responsible for intimidating Saddam's critics in the early days of the Iraqi leader's rise to power. The propaganda chief would later become famous for his ability to overlook advancing US forces and for his colorful vocabulary. To al-Sahaf, American troops were always "imperial mercenaries," "criminals" or "desert animals" who were always far away, even when they were inside Baghdad's city limits.

The start of the war also made me busier than I'd ever been in my life. Like the other networks, ABC switched to continuous live coverage, and I was on air every moment I could be. ABC, however, initially had trouble figuring out how to describe me. At first the anchors made sure to identify me as a "freelance reporter." My assumption at the time was that the network wanted to maintain distance from me in case I was killed. After a few days, however, the network embraced me, calling me "ABC's Richard Engel" and "our" correspondent. It felt good to finally be loved.

Day Two (March 20, 03)

More air strikes of about the same intensity of the first night. They were closer tonight. I could see fireballs after missiles hit the city across the river. I could smell burning buildings. I could hear planes passing very quickly overhead at high altitude, but the Pentagon is still only talking about cruise missiles. I'm not sure what's been destroyed.

Again on the second night, I watched the sound and light show from my balcony. I sat on a tank of gasoline (not the safest perch), talking on the sat phone as the Americans airmailed explosives to Baghdad and Iraqi anti-aircraft guns sprayed flak at them, as effective as spitballs. When the exchanges got especially heavy—*pound, pound, crackle, crackle*—I put on my flak jacket and helmet, the letters TV taped across it in an effort to limit those intentionally shooting at me to haters of the media. During the day, I'd been broadcasting from IHA's camera

fixed to the second-story roof of the press center. It was trans-
mitting live pictures as I spoke via sat phone from the hotel.
Although I was only separated from the camera by a couple of
miles, I suspect it may have been somewhat confusing to view-
ers, because I was describing one perspective of the city under
attack while the camera was showing another. I wouldn't go
near the press center at night, believing it would soon be transformed into a heap of rubble.

For the second night in a row, I was awake nearly all night
broadcasting via the sat phone or talking to editors in New
York, which is how I received nearly all of my information
about the war outside Baghdad. I also listened to my tiny,
made-in-China shortwave radio (a bargain at $7) and local
Iraqi radio and television. I was otherwise cut off from the US
war coverage, of which I am glad. All I knew for certain was
what I was able to see and hear.

On the second night of the war I watched the presidential palace compound across the Tigris—a sprawling complex of buildings spread out over a mile of riverbank—take
several direct hits. I also learned of the launch of the ground
offensive from Kuwait, and that some oil fires had been set.
It was all starting to happen. I was running on an adrenaline
buzz.

After sleeping about three hours, I met Ali the next morning. He'd brought the daily newspapers, freshly baked dia-
mond-shaped loaves of bread, white salty farmer's cheese and
a carton of mango juice. It was wonderful, and I ate as much
as I could both to settle my stomach, which was queasy from

stress and lack of sleep, and because I knew I'd have little time for foraging during the day.

Sahaf was in the middle of an angry tirade by the time I got to the press center. Evidently, US television had been broadcasting pictures of Iraqi soldiers surrendering in the South. Sahaf was livid.

"This is part of a media trick. . . . It's a game, an illusion!" he yelled. "Please be fair," he advised us. "That is all I ask. These are not Iraqi soldiers, but actors. Not a single Iraqi has surrendered to the imperial mercenaries. This is a ploy and it is failing miserably!" Sahaf concluded. "I can promise an assured death to any and all aggressors!" he added for good measure.

Later that day the Iraqi government vented its anger at the media by expelling the CNN team from Baghdad. I was told that Uday al-Ta'e (who later pointed the finger at Iraq's Deputy Prime Minister Tareq Aziz) had been personally incensed with CNN, accusing the network of warmongering. CNN correspondents Rym Brahimi and Nic Robertson and their teams were sent packing in a fury. I felt sorry for them. Although I hadn't seen CNN's coverage, I doubted it was any worse from Iraq's perspective than what I'd been saying on air. I'd called Saddam Hussein a dictator, I'd talked about the fear and repression he imposed and the mood in Iraq. CNN, however, could be seen locally. Uday watched CNN, FOX and BBC in his office. Luckily for me, Uday couldn't see ABC. After CNN's departure, Peter Arnett—working as a freelancer for NBC—and I were the only American television correspondents left in Baghdad. Arnett was something of a legend in Iraq. All the Iraqi officials knew him from the first Gulf War, which he'd covered for CNN. His familiarity with the regime, however, would ultimately be his downfall.

Sahaf was also vehemently decrying Washington's seizure of nearly two billion dollars in Iraqi assets in the United States. It was "thievery and plunder!" he declared. He also confirmed the attempt on Saddam's life, but that "God's hand protected him."

As I headed up to file my report from the live camera position, I was listening to Iraqi state radio on my Chinese shortwave. Saddam Hussein was offering an odd incentive plan, which I thought exposed Sahaf's claim that Iraqi soldiers were determined never to surrender. The radio broadcast said Saddam Hussein was personally offering the dinar equivalent of $40,000 to any Iraqi who shot down an enemy fighter jet, $20,000 for the downing of a US or British helicopter, $20,000 for the capture of an enemy soldier, and $10,000 for killing a US or British soldier. Foreign journalists weren't mentioned on the hit list. It seemed contradictory to me that Sahaf had accused US troops of being mercenaries while it was Iraq that was trying to buy the loyalty of its own forces.

The radio also quoted Uday Saddam Hussein as saying, "the wives and mothers of those Americans who fight us will cry blood instead of tears. They should not pretend that they will have a safe spot inside Iraq or outside of it!" I wondered why he said, "or outside of it." Was he threatening terrorism?

After filing live broadcasts for much of the morning and afternoon for *Good Morning America*, I headed to the Flowers Land to see Mohammed. I wanted to make sure he was still there. Instead I saw Zafar sitting on a couch in the lobby.

"What are you doing here?" I screamed at him. "I'm paying you to be at the hotel! Why else did I get you a room?"

"I didn't think you needed me anymore. I haven't heard from you in two days," he said, sulking.

"And you won't hear from me. All I want you to do is stay there. Just sit there in case I need you. Can't you do that?"

Zafar pursed his lips, lowered his head, and slunk out like a scolded child as I marched him back to his hotel. The policeman answered the door in an undershirt when we showed up. I couldn't smell the whiskey on his breath, but I could see his brain swimming behind his tired droopy eyes. And this was one of my safe houses.

I rushed back to the Palestine to start filing for that night's broadcasts. I wasn't frightened at this stage by the war. In fact, I was emboldened by the first two nights. I thought that if what I'd seen was all the US had in mind for the war, I'd been worrying too much.

Day Three—Shock and Awe (March 22, 03)

It was ten times the intensity of the first two nights.
The palace complex on the west side of the river, Al-Kasr al-Jumhuri, was smashed. I could feel the heat and wind of

the blasts against my face. I've gone three days almost
without sleep. I've been on air almost 24 hours a day.
Officials from the press center have been going through the
hotel looking for sat phones. I'm keeping mine under the bed.
    It felt like an earthquake when the bombs were dropping.
About half of the journalists slept in the shelter downstairs.
The bombs were falling one after another. It was like lightning
hitting the ground, the fury of Thor and Zeus crackling with
explosions.

From my perch it looked to me as if all of downtown Baghdad
was being destroyed. There was no moon in the sky (the air
campaign was timed to begin with the new moon to protect
against anti-aircraft fire) and it was a perfectly clear black
night, which made the explosions stand out in crisp contrast.
The bombs had been close enough that I could feel their hot
wind and the blast waves blew back my hair and pushed the
air out of my lungs.

    The entire western bank of the city where government
ministries were located was hit by what seemed like countless
bombs and cruise missiles. I watched the area disappear in
white smoke. It looked as if Baghdad were being eaten by a
cloud. I cannot exaggerate how terrifying it was. I thought
half the city was being flattened, leveled, eliminated.

When I emerged from the hotel the next morning, I felt like I'd
been out all night drinking, gotten into a bar fight, embar-

rassed myself, antagonized my friends and smacked a policeman. I was treading very lightly, worried the world was after
me. My legs were weak and I was on my best behavior, like a
child trying to avoid punishment. I didn't want to be caught. I
didn't want to be seen. I didn't know what I'd find in Baghdad
that morning, or what to say to the people I met. I didn't know
if there were hundreds, or even thousands, of people who'd
been killed overnight.

I was greatly relieved to find Ali waiting for me downstairs
in the hotel lobby with fresh bread, juice and cheese. He was
remarkably calm. He also had the morning newspapers in
hand. I was astonished that they'd managed to come out. It
was a sign that Baghdad was still standing. The newspapers
would continue to be published until the last day of the war.
As we drove around I was stunned by how little damage I
could actually see. I'd expected Baghdad to have become a
moonscape. Several buildings had been reduced to dust, and
most of the windows in the downtown area were shattered,
but the city was still recognizable.

I drove past several telephone exchanges that had been
reduced to smoldering hills of crumpled concrete with yellow
chunks of insulation hanging from twisted steel reinforcement
bars. Most of the destruction, however, had taken place behind
the high walls of presidential palaces and security compounds,
which had taken an incredible beating.

Ali was more shaken than he let on. He told me a cruise
missile had soared over his house. He'd watched it go overhead.

Ali's parents had fled Baghdad that morning to stay with relatives in a nearby rural village.

After spending the afternoon broadcasting, I asked the network for a few hours off. I needed to collect my thoughts, eat a proper meal and reassure Ali that I wouldn't abandon him. I took Ali to Zafar's favorite restaurant, the one I remembered for its "Sauce" and wonderful *kouzi*. I didn't expect to find anyone inside, but the place was teeming with customers. The headwaiter had to look to find us a table in the back.

While we were eating, the air campaign started up for the first time during the day. I could hear the thundering of the big firecrackers and missiles falling, destroying buildings and everything in them. But no one in the restaurant flinched. I tried to focus on the hum of conversations coming from other tables. People weren't even talking about the war unfolding around them. It was a bizarre moment. Bombs were exploding around us after a night of the most awesome air strikes Iraq had ever known, the government was under attack, American troops were advancing toward the capital, yet people were busy munching on meat, bread and hummos, seemingly oblivious to it all.

I think the attitude was the result of the psychological trauma Iraqis had been subjected to during the decades of Saddam Hussein's misrule. Iraqis had been so beaten down that they'd become ambivalent, like those bureaucrats I'd encountered with stares like prisoners on death row. In Iraq, it was considered unpatriotic to notice the war, and treasonous to discuss it, let alone speculate about the outcome. It was safer to just pretend not to notice what was going on, keep your head down, and wait for the storm to blow over. I found it very sad to see what years of dictatorship can do to the human soul.

CHAPTER FIVE

I WAS STANDING ON my balcony on the fourteenth floor of the Palestine Hotel when I saw the first plume of smoke emerge on the horizon like a black snake rising up from the desert. I thought a fire was roaring out of control about five miles away from me in the northern part of the city. It was mid-afternoon and the smoke was billowing hundreds of feet into the blue cloudless sky.

US and British forces had already dropped dozens of bombs around the edges of Baghdad that day, creating a steady pounding sound. Unlike the bombs that occasionally fell close to the Palestine, the distant explosions didn't crackle or snap or shake the hotel. Instead, they sang in deep bass tones, like fists punching a slab of beef.

I assumed the smoke was spewing from an Iraqi building,

munitions dump or fuel depot that had been turned into a smoldering parking lot and didn't worry about it too much. In less than a week, my tolerance for fires and explosions had grown to alarming proportions. I would no longer telephone the ABC News desk every time the bombings started. I would have been on the sat phone all day long. The air raids would start, stop and start again all day and night. I was surprised at how quickly I'd become accustomed to the air campaign and the war in general. I'd seen Israelis and Palestinians both quickly acclimate to an environment of extreme violence, but until it happened to me, I didn't quite understand how easy it was. The last time I'd seen it was a year earlier among Palestinian boys in the West Bank.

In March 2002, the Israeli army launched Operation Defensive Shield in response to the horrific Passover-night suicide attack in Netanya near Tel Aviv. Not only was it the bloodiest suicide attack yet of the new Palestinian intifada but it was carried out on a Jewish holiday. Israel had to respond.

Operation Defensive Shield, however, was only defensive to those who believe that a strong offense is the best defense. Within days of its outset, the campaign grew into the largest military operation in the Palestinian territories since the 1967 Middle East War. Israeli troops recaptured every major city on the West Bank except for the tiny oasis of Jericho, which was already isolated from Israel by a deep valley and desert. Scores of Palestinians were killed each day, as were many Israeli soldiers, especially in the northern West Bank city of Jenin, where Palestinians accused Israeli forces of a massacre after they leveled a section of the city while people were still in their homes. Israel subsequently blocked a UN investigating team from carrying out fieldwork in the area. In response to Operation Defensive Shield, Palestinian groups including Hamas, Islamic Jihad and the Al-Aqsa Martyrs Brigade unleashed everything they had, and bombs were exploding across Israel every week. I lost a neighbor—a father of two and a great believer in reconciliation between Israelis and Arabs—and a friend narrowly escaped death in a trendy café that was blown apart by a radical Palestinian who evidently believed he would become a martyr to his people and Islam if he killed innocent people. My friend temporarily lost his hearing from the café explosion, but emerged without so much as a cut or bruise. People around him were killed. It was a time of sheer ugliness on both sides.

About three weeks into Operation Defensive Shield, I was able to enter the West Bank city of Ramallah. At the time, the Israeli army was regularly denying foreign reporters access to the re-occupied Palestinian cities, declaring them "closed military zones."

Ramallah was under curfew. I walked through the city, cautiously peering around corners from the shelter of doorways and private homes.

I watched a group of Palestinian boys about junior-high-school age run up behind an Israeli Merkava tank, jump onto its back and take a joyride for about a hundred yards before leaping off to the cheers of their friends. It was the stupidest, most risky thing I'd seen anyone do. A Palestinian friend told me it was the latest test of bravery, and a way to impress girls. Anyone who has ever seen a moving tank (and Israeli Merkavas are very big menacing tanks) up close can understand the incredible bravado it would take to hop onto one of those modern-day dragons.

While I wasn't yet ready for tank surfing, I'd come to see the bombings in Baghdad as like a thunderstorm, noisy and powerful but not necessarily dangerous. This would change later in the week, when I saw just what happened to people who got caught in the storm.

I counted about twenty plumes of black smoke in the circle around Baghdad. One fire had also popped up near the Palestine and I could see the orange flames belching raven smoke. It was obvious oil was burning, and it was releasing caustic fumes that burned my eyes and throat. The Iraqi government had set hundreds of oil fires all over Baghdad to create a ring of smoke, a black hand to cloak the city. Although many American military commentators—the so-called armchair generals—dismissed the effectiveness of the smokescreen (a tactic favored by the Soviet military doctrine that had guided the Iraqi military for decades) and rightly pointed out that it was useless to stop GPS guided missiles, the black clouds did present problems for weapons like the Predator—an unmanned

drone that hunted by sight over Iraq, waiting for the chance to
take out Saddam Hussein or his top associates. I've since seen
satellite photographs of Baghdad taken during the war and
there were portions of the city that couldn't be seen because of
the smoke, making it somewhat easier for Saddam Hussein to
move around in stealth.

The next morning, Ali arrived at the hotel about an hour
later than usual. He'd been searching the city for fresh bread
and cheese for our breakfast. Nearly all of the bakeries and
grocers were closed, and the few still open had dramatically
raised prices.

We drove up to one small grocery, a single narrow room
packed with cigarettes, candy, soft drinks, canned meats,
canned beans and bags of pasta and rice, and I asked the shop
owner about his prices.

"Prices . . . same, same," he told me. "Iraq same, same.
Saddam Hussein good."

I'd forgotten Iraq was still pretending there wasn't a war
going on. I remembered announcements I'd heard on local
radio stations calling for Iraqis to live life as normal. The broadcasts stressed that the government hadn't imposed a curfew
and that people were free to go outside, in fact encouraged to
take walks and go to work, although government jobs and
schools were temporarily closed for "security reasons."
Although I don't know if it was because of the radio campaign,
life in Baghdad did have a surprisingly "normal" feel about it.

At the Baath party checkpoints all over the city, for example, the militiamen just stood at their posts like traffic cops on perpetual coffee breaks, loitering with their Kalashnikovs slung loosely over their shoulders, chitchatting and smoking cigarettes. I even saw some of them laughing and horsing around, chasing each other like boys in a locker room. After a few days, I hardly noticed the militiamen anymore. They'd become Baghdad wallpaper.

Ali told me the grocer had been defensive because he didn't want to give the impression that he was taking advantage of the hard times to jack up prices, although that's exactly what was happening. A fifty-cent carton of eggs now suddenly cost the equivalent of two dollars, and a can of sweetened condensed milk (which I bought to add to the Nescafé I made every night in a hotpot in my room) cost about five dollars, more than twice what I'd paid a week earlier.

Making matters worse for many Iraqis was that shop owners were no longer extending credit. It's still fairly common in the Arab world for customers to pay their bills at the end of the month. These days, store owners wanted cash up front.

Food was nonetheless still plentiful in Baghdad. Bread prices were unchanged, and open markets continued to overflow with apples, bananas, guavas, tomatoes and onions that were amazingly cheap. Inflation seemed mainly to have affected prepackaged and canned goods and, for some odd reason, eggs.

And I was surprised to discover that the Iraqi dinar had gained slightly against the dollar since the days immediately following President Bush's ultimatum. There was no longer a rush on dollars, nor a drive to sell them. The economy was essentially at a standstill and the currency had stabilized in paralysis.

After our little shopping trip, Ali and I headed to the press center. We found it in chaos. More than a hundred people were running toward a nearby bridge over the Tigris. An Iraqi claimed to have seen two American pilots eject from a plane and land in the river. A mob was swelling by the riverbank. People were searching for the pilots through the reeds growing along the water's edge. Soldiers were firing into the river and setting the brush on fire to destroy any possible hiding place. I fully expected the Iraqis to do something barbaric to the pilots if they found them. I do not think Iraqis are savages, and have found the people to be extremely kindhearted, but mobs are insane, and frustrated mobs are much worse, especially when a population feels powerless and threatened. I have seen Palestinians, for example, drag the bodies of Israeli collaborators through the streets of Bethlehem and hang them upside down in Manger Square as a warning to others. I was bracing for a similarly horrific scene.

I ran to the edge of the bridge and, leaning over shoulders of Iraqi youths, looked down at the water but didn't see any pilots.

An American jet roared through the sky overhead, throwing the impassioned mob into a panic. People started to scatter in all directions. Someone was yelling that the fighter was going to blow up the bridge to help the pilots escape. Everyone began to run. There were cars crossing the bridge, too, speeding to escape. It was pandemonium. People jumped into cars and drove away frantically. One car nearly ran me over. I'd been searching for Ali among the crowd and the driver had been watching the chaotic scene, calling out questions to people as he drove forward. I only saw him when he was nearly on top of me. I dove off the road onto the sidewalk of the bridge and banged my knee on the pavement. The driver never even slowed down. I found Ali and limped off the bridge as quickly as possible. I wanted out of there: I was an American, limping and wearing a khaki, safari-style shirt that could possibly have looked like part of a military uniform. I worried that some excited Iraqi would point to me and say, "There's the pilot!"

The jet made several more passes. Iraqi air defenses started firing anti-aircraft guns from the roof of a nearby building. The short bursts of gunfire sounded like the loud croaking of angry frogs.

After my next broadcast, I ran into Abu Annas, who told me that the information minister and the Iraqi vice president, Taha Yasin Ramadan, were giving a briefing. Ramadan was bragging that Iraqi forces had captured several American soldiers when I got there. He said Iraqi television would broadcast their pictures later that day. Ramadan also made what I believe was the first direct call from a senior Iraqi official for a global jihad against Americans.

"Every Arab and Muslim around the world should be a bullet directed at the chest of the enemy until the aggressors leave the lands of the Arabs and Islam," he said.

It was a step beyond Saddam's call on Iraqis to fight a jihad against the invading American forces. Technically, from a Muslim perspective, Iraq was fighting a legitimate jihad. Most moderate Muslim preachers and scholars describe jihad as a war of self-defense in which Muslims are duty bound to fight against non-Muslim invaders. Ramadan, however, was calling for a holy war more along the lines of what Osama bin Laden supports—one in which Muslims from around the world are asked to participate in a struggle they're not directly involved in. Bin Laden, coincidentally, believes his jihad is defensive in nature—under threat from "Crusaders and Jews" (i.e., the United States and Israel)—but is also a believer in that precarious theory of the offensive defense. So, by the way, is the Bush administration.

Then it was al-Sahaf's turn. "They (the Americans) said it would be shock and awe, but they are in shock and in awe of Iraq's resistance.

"The Baath party has seven million fighters and they are in every appropriate place. We will keep them in awe. Um Kasr was just a little taste."

American and British forces had just entered the southern port city of Um Kasr and fighting had been intense by all accounts. The Americans had initially said they'd taken control of Um Kasr, but later qualified the claim.

"The American-Zionist schemes will not be carried out,"

al-Sahaf declared. "The White House is a black house that wants to bring death to every place.

"Our forces destroyed four enemy tanks and killed enemy forces. The rest of the imperialist mercenaries fled like rats. Our militias are now surrounding those rats."

It was typical al-Sahaf, a mixture of lies and truth wrapped in bombast and colorful insults. I didn't know what to believe and what to ignore.

That night Iraqi television did indeed broadcast footage of American POWs. The TV newscast began with the usual playing of the Iraqi national anthem, then a young TV presenter in a military uniform said, "Tonight we will broadcast pictures of dead American, British and Zionist forces."

ABC, and other American networks, had decided not to broadcast the pictures and accused Iraq of violating the Geneva Convention by exploiting POWs for propaganda. On the other hand, al-Jazeera and many European TV networks did show the images of the American prisoners. They were powerful and disturbing, and brought home the idea that American kids were fighting so far from home.

Iraqi television first showed pictures of a blood-splattered supply truck, marked, in English, POTABLE WATER. It was parked in the middle of a desert road. The truck's driver, a soldier in an American uniform, was slumped dead out his window. One side of his head was bloodied and black from burns. There was another dead soldier in uniform flat on his back on the road. The camera moved inside a room, where I counted six bodies haphazardly piled on top of one another on the floor as if they'd been carelessly dumped there. The camera closed in on the smashed head of one of the soldiers.

"Look at these bodies, Mr. Bush and Mr. Blair," the announcer said as the camera panned over the gory scene. "We are people of culture and we didn't attack you, but this is what awaits those who attack Iraq."

The television then aired brief interviews with five American POWs. The soldiers—four men and a woman—were being held in a white room that looked like it could have been a prison cell or even a hospital room. Several of the prisoners were wearing bandages. An unseen interviewer put a microphone in front of each POW, asking the prisoner to state his name, hometown and age for the camera.

The first soldier—a young man with a crew cut, round eyeglasses and a green T-shirt—was visibly shaken. He had trouble understanding the interviewer's broken English questions, and kept looking at another person off camera for help. Another prisoner was then interviewed while supine on his back in a bed. He was clearly in pain and had blood on his T-shirt and a bandage around his bicep.

"This is a message to the American people that your soldiers will pay a heavy price," the announcer continued. "This is what is waiting for them."

My heart went out to the soldiers who'd died and those who'd lost their freedom. I wondered what would happen to the POWs once the war turned. So far, government officials like al-Sahaf and Ramadan seemed confident, even cocky. As long as they stayed that way, I felt, the POWs were probably safe. But what would happen to them (and me) once the regime felt it was fighting for its survival?

I think Iraqi officials at this stage of the war really believed they were going to win. Al-Sahaf relished that a US soldier had thrown grenades at his fellow troops in Kuwait, telling me after the press conference that it was a sign the Americans were "divided over their unjust war."

Uday al-Ta'e also seemed relaxed, and would strut around the press center, amicably chatting with foreign reporters and overseeing builders who were doing renovation work, sanding and shaping a new stone façade for the building that would be bombed a few days later.

The Iraqi government was especially pleased that a major sandstorm was whipping through the South and heading toward Baghdad. In what had become daily televised speeches, Saddam Hussein described the sandstorm as a gift from God to the Iraqi people.

The sandstorm hit Baghdad full force on the morning of March 26, blanketing the city in a layer of grit as fine as powdered sugar. The sand was so light, in fact, that it stayed suspended in the air, turning the sky bright orange. I'd never seen such a sandstorm in seven years in the Middle East. Iraqis said it was the most intense *asifa* they'd had in a generation. Cars were covered in what looked like orange snow.

The theater of war now truly looked like a theater, complete with stage lighting. Oil fires were still burning, sending black plumes rising into what looked like a flaming sky. Shakespeare couldn't have scripted a more dramatic backdrop for war, which was about to meet the people of Baghdad face on.

I was at the press center, covering my mouth with a handkerchief to block out the smoke and sand, when Abu Annas told me the Americans had just bombed a market, killing at least a dozen people. I was skeptical. Al-Sahaf and other officials had talked ad nauseam about civilian casualties, but I hadn't yet seen any. I'd witnessed injured people in hospitals, but couldn't confirm what had hurt them; I suspected falling Iraqi anti-aircraft fire may in fact have been the cause. The Iraqi government had also organized tours for us to see bomb damage, but we only saw empty broken buildings. They always took us to sites that had been hit at least twenty-four hours earlier, but this time Abu Annas said there was a bus leaving right away. I didn't want to ride the bus. Earlier that morning I'd been on a bus tour to visit sites (always civilian sites) that had been destroyed. The Iraqi authorities never took the reporters to the military installations that had been attacked. While we'd been on the bus, we'd heard jets roaring overhead and then the concussion of their bombs. The Americans couldn't have known that the bus I was on was full of reporters. We asked the driver to pull off the road, but he kept going. The jet made another pass—*boom boom boom*. We started yelling at the driver to go

back to the press center, but he ignored us, insisting on contin-
uing to the next stop, a hospital where we were scheduled to
listen to a speech by the health minister. After that, I decided
I'd had enough of government-run bus tours. I didn't want to
be trapped in Iraqi hands again.

Abu Annas reluctantly agreed to let me go in Ali's Toyota
Super to the market he said had just been bombed. Of course,
he insisted on coming with us.

Ali and I were silent on the way to the al-Shaab neighborhood, about ten miles outside the city center. I didn't want Abu
Annas to know how friendly Ali and I had become. I was filming the city with a mini-DV camera as we drove by oil fires and
checkpoints. Abu Annas seemed somewhat uncomfortable that
I was filming, but didn't object. Instead he instructed Ali to take
a more circuitous route to the al-Shaab area that took us around
several military buildings the Americans had destroyed.

When we arrived at the al-Shaab neighborhood I jumped
out of the car, and Abu Annas never made any attempt to follow me. It had started to rain and he evidently didn't want to
dirty his corduroy suit. Ali stayed with him in the car, leaving
me to wander alone. The Iraqi minder system often worked out
that way. It seemed oppressive, and the minders always needed
to be taken into consideration, but with a little luck and energy
the minders—most of them lazy—could often be overcome.
Lorenzo Cremonesi, an Italian journalist who works for *Cor-
riere della Sera* and does triathlons in his spare time, had taught
me a trick to beat the minders during my previous trip to Iraq.

"Pick the fat ones," he advised, "and then walk them to death." After a few hours of walking, he said, the minders—most of whom were also chain smokers—inevitably excused themselves to go home for "an important family matter."

Abu Annas was in good physical condition, but his weakness was that he didn't like to get dirty. It was enough. Each minder only needed one flaw to be beaten.

The al-Shaab area wasn't exactly a market but a low-end commercial district. We'd parked along a wide street lined with shops selling water heaters, pipes and kitchen sinks. There were two craters, one on each side of the road. The missiles had destroyed several shops and the apartments above them. One of the blasts had tossed a car onto the sidewalk, where it lay mangled and flipped on its back like a dead crab on a beach. The rain started to pick up, and I was quickly covered in the orange sand the rain was pulling from the sky. My notebook from that day was covered in so much wet sand that I had to wipe the pages clean with the back of my hand to read what I'd written. Later, I wrote in my journal what I'd seen.

March 26, 2003

I saw a man pick through the rubble. He uncovered a severed hand under a board. He picked it up by a finger and held it up over his head. Everyone started cheering, "Allahu Akhbar! Allahu Akhbar!"

There were pools of blood in the mud beneath my feet. I was walking through the mud, trying to avoid stepping in the blood. I didn't want to offend people by walking in the blood. But I couldn't avoid it.

I saw a nearly intact brain on the cement floor inside one of the shops. It was nauseating. The atmosphere was tense.

It was in fact very tense.

"This is the blood of Iraqi civilians! This is the blood of the Iraqi people," a man yelled in my face as I walked through the bloody pool mixed with mud. He bent down and put his hands in the blood and then shoved his hands in my face so I could see it close up. He was both crying and yelling at the same time. I tried to back away, but found myself surrounded by people cheering, "Allahu Akhbar!" Arabic for *God is Greatest*. The phrase is the heart of the prayers pious Muslims perform five times a day. It embodies everything Muslims believe, which is fundamentally that God—Allah—is greater than human existence and that a Muslim—a word that literally means in Arabic a person who "surrenders"—must submit to God's greater power. Calling out *Allahu Akhbar* was a way for the crowd to try to overcome the tragedy—which they were powerless to prevent—by drawing strength from their faith. To call out *Allahu Akhbar* meant—perhaps subconsciously—that they would not be defeated because God's power is greater than what had just happened, greater than death or American bombs. I'd seen Palestinians react similarly to death many, many times. Allahu Akhbar! Today you killed me, but remember, God is greatest.

I tried to back out of the circle of people around me.

"Why are the Americans bombing during the day?" one man yelled at me. "Bush promised not to target civilians, but these were all civilians! What did these people do?"

The crowd continued to grow. People were all shouting at once. They knew I was a reporter because I was carrying a camera and a notebook. Luckily, no one knew I was an American. These people had just lost family members, neighbors and friends. I beefed up my Egyptian accent, making sure to pronounce my J's like G's and use colloquial expressions common in the Egyptian dialect, which all Iraqis recognize from Egyptian movies and TV sitcoms.

"How could the Americans see what they were hitting through the sandstorm?" another man demanded that I explain to him.

I think the most revealing question—which wasn't really a question, but was an example of the Arab use of rhetorical questions—was "If the Americans didn't want to hit civilians, why did they hit civilians?"

I suggested that perhaps the bombing had been a mistake. Everyone around me emphatically shook his head to say "no way." People were convinced that what had happened could not have been a mistake, although they had no way of knowing that. I've found this attitude common in the Arab world. I believe it stems from a combination of the general mistrust of the American government with a reverence for, and faith in, American (and Israeli) technology. It was the same attitude I found in many Arab countries after the atrocities of September 11, 2001, which many people in the Middle East continue to believe were launched by a Jewish conspiracy. Many Arabs had such esteem for the CIA, the Mossad and American military gadgetry—their impressions reinforced by Hollywood action movies popular in the region—that they refused to believe the Americans could have let the World Trade Center and the Pentagon be attacked if they didn't want it to happen. It was the same attitude I was finding in Iraq. The Iraqis had seen American cruise missiles turn corners in mid-flight and destroy government ministry buildings without scratching the paint of adjacent homes and therefore believed President Bush's promise of a war that would target Saddam Hussein and spare the Iraqi people. Yet two missiles had just landed in the middle of a poor commercial area. The people wanted to know why. They concluded that the Americans must have planned it that way and felt they'd been lied to.

I asked people in the huddle around me what interest the United States would have in bombing a civilian neighborhood. "They want to break the backs of the Iraqi people . . . to break our will. But we will never be broken!" one man shouted. People liked his answer and started cheering, "Allahu Akhbar, Allahu Akhbar!"

The Pentagon later tried to distance itself from the al-Shaab bombing, saying "it did not target civilians" and that it was "quite possible" that the blasts could have been caused by Iraqi missiles.

I don't know what caused the blasts. I do know, however,

that the Iraqi government did capitalize on the attack for its propaganda. The next day, Iraqi newspapers published large color pictures of the casualties on both their front and back covers. The images were shockingly gruesome: closeups of severed limbs and nearly decapitated bodies.

Forty-eight hours after the missile strikes in the al-Shaab district, two more missiles landed during the evening shopping hours in a poor open market in Baghdad. This time more than sixty Iraqi civilians were killed. I saw food stalls splattered with blood. Raw sewage was pouring out of broken pipes in the ground. My pants and shoes were covered in filth as I trudged through the aftermath. After the second attack, no one in Baghdad believed that only Saddam Hussein and his government were the targets of the American war.

As I stood in the al-Shaola market—the scene of the second attack—a crowd gathered around me. Again, men were screaming in my ears. "The Americans have high-tech weapons," one man yelled. "They know what they hit. They wanted to hit us!"

"This is not about Saddam Hussein," added another man. "Even if the Americans remove him we'll continue to fight. This is a war against Islam. A true Arab never bows his head to the enemy, but looks up to God."

CHAPTER SIX

O N MARCH 29 IT FINALLY happened. The American and British forces—I always felt uncomfortable calling only two countries "a coalition"—bombed the Information Ministry in the middle of the night. I wasn't sorry to see it hit, but it did leave me without a place to work. The morning after the air strike, Ali and I drove to the press center—both out of curiosity and force of habit. We knew the building had become a target, but I was tied to it. The live TV cameras were still at the building, and so were the minders. The press center had become my "home away from home," although it seemed more like an orphanage run by a bunch of lackeys who worked for a hateful government.

The Information Ministry building looked relatively intact when we pulled up to it. The building—like the Palestine—consisted of a tall tower that rose from a wider base, making it look something like a two-tiered wedding cake, albeit one designed in a stark, socialist architectural style. The press center had been in the bottom layer of the cake. The tower had housed the offices where information minister Uday al-Ta'e and the other spies worked and, I presume, played too. The American bombs had punched a hole in the middle of the tower's roof, shredding Iraqi TV satellite dishes that had perched there. The bomb had exploded after it was in the middle of the tower, blowing out the offices and ultimately shattering most of the windows. Parts of the building had evidently caught fire and there were black lick marks above many windows. Amazingly, the live TV cameras—located above the press center, on the flat of the first step of the "wedding cake"—were left relatively unscathed.

Although the sandstorm had by now mostly dissipated, it had covered every surface with fine orange powder. The storm's ferocious winds had also thrown our tripods, tents, windscreens and other assorted gear every which way.

I was plugged in to my live camera—weighted down by sandbags—waiting for my turn on *Good Morning America*, when I heard a fighter jet rip through the sky overhead. It was an American jet. I say this with confidence because as far as I am aware, the Iraqi air force never got off the ground. In fact, Iraqi planes were found after the war buried in the desert, some wrapped in plastic, others simply covered in sand. The Iraqis either didn't want to lose their prized jets or thought it would have been suicide to go up in them. I tore off my microphone and ran out of the building, fearing the American jet was preparing to finish the work of the previous night and flatten the Information Ministry. All the journalists had congregated in the parking lot, watching the plane carve a white trail high over our heads. After ten minutes, however, we started inching back to our posts. Most of us had some faith that the Americans wouldn't bomb the press center in the middle of the day. The Iraqis were evidently counting on it, because moments before my live shot was supposed to come up I heard another jet soar overhead, followed by the burping of anti-aircraft fire, the croaking bursts so close and loud that my knees instinctively buckled, sending me into a tight defensive crouch. The anti-aircraft fire was coming from directly above our heads. The Iraqis had put an anti-aircraft gun on the upper roof of the Information Ministry and were shooting over us. In essence, the reporters had become human shields providing cover to that anti-aircraft position. I didn't want to protect the Information Ministry, nor the gunner, with my body. All I wanted to do was finish my two-way with *Good Morning America*, unplug, get off the roof and head back to the Palestine.

The anti-aircraft gun fired several more times while I waited to come up in the rundown. I worried that if the bullets even came close to hitting the jet, or if the pilot just got too annoyed by the threatening fire, I would have been, to use one of my favorite colloquialisms, toast. The wait was agonizing and I stood on the balcony like a boy waiting to use the bathroom, hopping from one foot to the other.

That was, thankfully, the last time I reported from the

press center. Luckily, the Iraqis didn't want to be in the press center any more than the journalists did and had started packing up their files and carting away office furniture. Uday al-Ta'e allowed anyone who still had a camera in Baghdad to move it from the Information Ministry to the Palestine. The rest of the day was pandemonium as we scrambled to haul away our equipment before sundown, when we thought the press center would be hit again.

The Palestine was now our home base, where we slept, worked and, unfortunately, ate most of our meals. After the press center was destroyed, the minders moved into the Palestine and Uday al-Ta'e set up an office in the lobby. He also became very strict, and said we weren't allowed to go anywhere without our minders, including out to eat, which left us with little choice but the Palestine's "Orient Express." Built in the late 1970s, the restaurant was appointed with dark wood and smoky glass to create an *ancien regime* train décor. Sketched on the restaurant's walls were the names of international tourist destinations, including PARIS, ROME and ISTANBUL. The tables, draped in white tablecloths, were lined up in rows to resemble a train's dining car. The restaurant wasn't altogether ugly and it did have some nostalgic appeal, but the chef was arguably the most unimaginative person on earth. He served almost exactly the same meal every single night: spaghetti with tomato sauce (sometimes varied with penne in tomato sauce), broiled chicken and stewed zucchini. The repetitive menu wasn't for a lack of fresh produce in Baghdad; every day, I passed markets chock full of explosively ripe tomatoes, eggplants of assorted colors and sizes, fresh meat, poultry and fruit of every flavor. Yet even when the world seemed like it was coming to an end, our chef was never inspired.

The Palestine was now filled with roughly one hundred foreign reporters, cameramen and photographers and about fifty minders and assorted press center officials. It was a bizarre sleepover party with terrible catering. Fortunately for me, however, Abu Annas didn't want to leave his wife and daughter at home alone, which meant he returned to his house every night, leaving me with more freedom than most reporters. During the day, Abu Annas would sit in his brown corduroy suit on a couch in the hotel lobby waiting for me to go outside. If I went out the back door, I was free to roam the city as I pleased; or at least that's what I thought.

After reporting about the previous night's bombings— which like clockwork chimed all night long for what was to be twenty straight days—I headed out the back door, successfully evading Abu Annas, who never left his couch. He was an anomaly among minders. He didn't smoke, drink tea, or as far as I know, ever go to the bathroom. Ali was waiting for me outside and we set out with my mini-DV camera. I was excited to be alone, hopeful I'd get raw opinions.

I first talked to a fruit seller who invited me to come to his home, but then turned me away after serving me a glass of sweet tea and swapping with me the customary religiously imbued persiflage: "May God give you good health," "God Willing" and "May God keep you." He told me his wife was uncomfortable with having me in the house. It was obvious that he and his wife were still too scared of the regime to talk. I understood their fears. He had nothing to gain and everything to lose by talking to me. I left bowing politely with my hand over my heart and drove to a nearby telephone exchange the Americans had obliterated. In Iraq, each neighborhood was serviced by a central telephone exchange through which all calls were routed. At least two four-thousand-pound bombs had plowed into this exchange. The blast had rocked the Palestine and shaken the windows in my room two days earlier. What was left was a twisted nest of torn wires and steel reinforcement bars from which bits of concrete dangled like Christmas ornaments; some of the destroyed telephone equipment was still ringing, giving the building an eerie sense of being alive, albeit slowly dying.

Baath party members surrounded me within less than two minutes of my arrival. Some were in green fatigues; others were dressed in civilian clothing. They were all carrying Kalashnikovs. I stuffed my DV camera into a carrying case over my shoulder, but it was too late—they'd seen me filming. The militiamen demanded to know who I was. I told them I was a journalist and showed them the press card I'd been issued by the Information Ministry. The man who appeared to be in charge studied the laminated card with my picture on it and demanded to see Ali's papers, which he handed to another Baath party member who put them in his pocket without looking at them.

"Where is your minder?" the leading Baath party member dressed in a camouflage jacket asked me.

Ali was surprisingly defiant and told them I was a journalist, insisting that I had the proper credentials and implying with the tone of his voice that they should buzz off.

I grabbed Ali's arm, sensing that if he tried to fight he would only make the situation worse.

The Baath party leader told Ali to follow him in his car to the police station. He was going to take us into custody. At the very least I was going to be expelled from Iraq, and at the worst—well—the worst could have happened. I didn't want to spend a single minute at an Iraqi security headquarters these days. They were being blown up day and night. The Baath party member who'd inspected my card started giving instructions to his colleagues on how they were to follow the "American" on the way to the police station. My nationality was written on my press card.

"Sir, you clearly know that I am a journalist," I told him in Arabic. "So why are you taking us in?"

"I don't know that. How can I be sure who you are?" he asked me. "Are you American or Egyptian?" he asked, picking up my accent.

"I'm American. It says so on my press card. Do you think if I had fake press credentials I would write on them that I was an American?"

He laughed, but then got deadly serious.

"If I see an American here on the streets in Baghdad I could kill him. You are an American, right?"

"Yes, but I'm a civilian," I said. "I'm a journalist just trying to do my job."

"We are all civilians," he shot back, raising his voice and waving his finger in the air. "I'm a civilian! The houses that the enemy Americans are destroying are civilian houses!"

"If you kill me," I said, trying to be as calm as I could, "who's going to tell the Iraqi people's story, just the reporters embedded with the US Army?"

"And do you tell the truth?" he asked me, and looked deeply into my eyes. I doubt he had any idea what journalists "embedded" with the military meant. I'm sure that as far as he was concerned, all American journalists were embedded with the American government, the same way Iraqi reporters took orders from their government. "Do you tell the truth about what's going on here?"

"I'm out here talking to you, aren't I? If I didn't want to talk to the Iraqis and tell the world what they're thinking then why would I be out on the streets—in Iraq—during wartime—talking to you?"

The rhetorical argument apparently worked, because he let us go. *Il hamdu Allah*, as people in the Arab world say. "Thank God."

I was delighted to see Abu Annas back at the Palestine. I was on my best behavior, somehow hoping that it would erase my little run-in with the Baath party irregulars. Word never got back to the Information Ministry officials about my wanderings, and Uday al-Ta'e actually started being very nice to me, although he always called me Michael. I never corrected him.

"Michael come with me," he said later that day as he toured the Palestine's lobby—his new kingdom—with me arm in arm, an Arab show of brotherly affection. He told me he'd arranged a meeting with Tareq Aziz, which I'd asked for a week earlier. Uday said I should be ready because the interview would take place in a few hours at a location I'd only learn about later.

I almost missed that interview with Tareq Aziz, which would ultimately be his last as Iraq's deputy prime minister. I only had my mini-DV camera and no crew. I would need two crews to do a proper television interview: one to film me, the other to film Aziz. As soon as Uday walked away I grabbed an Iraqi cameraman who'd been lingering in the lobby. He'd been freelancing for a Spanish television network. I begged him to let me hire him for a few hours. He wanted $500, and I wasn't in a position to argue. He told me he didn't have any lights, microphones or an extra tripod, and strolled off—too casually for my taste—to borrow the equipment from other camera-men friends of his. I had my doubts he'd be back in time. He was still gone when Uday came back.

"Come with me Michael and don't say anything," Uday said and led me to one of the Palestine Hotel's conference rooms. The huge room was empty except for two gold-painted chairs, which had been set up across from each other. There was an Iraqi flag behind one of the chairs and a small coffee table adorned with a vase of plastic flowers. But the room, equipped with only a few halogen lights shining high in the ceiling, was much too dark for an interview. I called in the hotel's engineer, who said he had some emergency lights in the basement. "Yalla, get going," Uday ordered, and the engineer rushed off. About ten minutes later he wheeled in a massive spotlight large enough to advertise the grand opening of a restaurant. I was afraid to shine this great buzzing beast on Aziz. We discovered, however, if we directed the light against the wall, its reflection was still bright enough for the interview. My cameraman finally arrived, a couple of minutes before Aziz walked into the room with al-Sahaf. They were both laughing. Aziz was wearing a green military uniform complete with a pistol in a belt holster.

"You ever use that?" I asked him jokingly.

"No, but at times like these you never know," he said amicably. Aziz seemed extremely confident and was quietly charming. He spoke very slowly in a low, self-assured voice, sounding a bit like Henry Kissinger.

I had the cameraman shoot Aziz and positioned my mini-DV facing me. I was holding a microphone in my lap. It was an altogether sloppy job, and I had no idea if my camera was even recording when we started to talk.

The chitchat I had with Aziz while we were setting up was perhaps the most revealing part of our discussion. I asked Aziz if he thought the war was going better than he'd expected.

"Yes, much better," he said, clearly expressing relief. But he then quickly caught himself and said, "Of course we always said this war would be a great disaster for the United States." It was obvious that Aziz, and I think all the senior Iraqi officials, were surprised that the regime was still intact ten days into the bombing campaign. The sandstorm had given Saddam's government a lease on life. The Americans' advance on Baghdad did seem to be slowing down, and there were US media reports of finger pointing in Washington about the apparent weakness of the war plan. There were open debates on American television that the Pentagon hadn't sent enough soldiers to do the job. It was all seen as a sign of weakness by the Saddam regime, which didn't publicize its dirty laundry, especially not potential flaws of its war plan while the war was still being fought.

I was very sick at this stage. I hadn't been getting much sleep, and my stomach—because of the stress, smoke in the air, lack of sleep and generally dirty conditions—was a disaster. But worst of all was my hacking cough. I couldn't take a deep breath without exploding into a hacking fit, which can be a problem if you're a broadcast journalist. About fifteen minutes into my interview with Aziz my cough got the better of me. I was coughing so loudly that I became totally redfaced and started crying. Aziz handed me his glass of water, which I could barely hold steady as I shook with painful coughs. I tearfully thanked Aziz for his time and said I couldn't go on, waving off the interview. Somewhat taken aback, Aziz stood up abruptly, extended his hand to me formally and turned to leave. I joked as he walked away with al-Sahaf that I was a new "American biological weapon." We all laughed and I coughed some more as they left the room.

It was this chummy relationship with representatives of an enemy government that got the better of Peter Arnett a few days later. Arnett, who was in the best position of any correspondent in Baghdad to cover the war, since he'd been one of only a handful of journalists who'd also reported on the first

Gulf War, had given an interview to Iraqi state television. In it, he said the American war plan had failed and cast doubt on the American people's support for the war. It was undoubtedly a stupid move. We all had our personal opinions—I was worried Washington didn't have a clear post-war plan—and we all did what we thought was necessary to butter up the Iraqi officials; after all, our lives were, in many ways, in their hands. I for one had treated Uday to several lunches and laughed at his jokes. But Arnett had gone a step further. He'd allowed himself to be used for Iraqi propaganda. A few hours after NBC—who'd contracted him for the war—fired him, Arnett told me that the interview had been "bad judgment."

"Richard, all I have to say to you is be careful," he told me. I tried to remember his advice.

Some of the journalists at the Palestine Hotel believed Arnett was a victim of American jingoism and taped up a sign in the lobby asking for protest signatures. While I didn't add my name to the list, I did feel sorry for Arnett. He was in the process of rebuilding a great career that had fallen. He was making a heroic comeback, only to fall because of hubris and bad judgment. It was a classic Greek tragedy. Amazingly, with Arnett off air, I became the only remaining American television correspondent in Baghdad. It gave me pause. While I understand why most of the journalists left during the buildup to the war, I've never quite understood why so many reporters and news agencies were surprised by the impending danger the war presented. The buildup to the war had taken months, and television networks had spent millions of dollars training staff and buying protective equipment, but when it came time to use it most people balked.

One thing no one could prepare for, however, was street-to-street guerilla war, which I feared had begun on March 29 when an Iraqi carried out a suicide attack against advancing American troops.

Ali Jafar al-No'mani, a father of five, blew up his car at a roadblock near Najaf—a city a hundred miles south of Baghdad holy to Shiite Muslims—killing four American servicemen. The Iraqi media showered al-No'mani with praise and Saddam promoted him posthumously from an Iraqi army warrant officer, a rank below officer, to a full colonel.

The next day a spokesman for the Iraqi army, General Hazem al-Rawi, said there were four thousand volunteer suicide bombers in Iraq from foreign countries in addition to the thousands of Iraqis, like al-No'mani, ready to die for their country. Iraq's bellicose vice president Taha Yasin Ramadan—the man who'd initially made an appeal for a global jihad—told reporters that the Americans, whom he described, "Sahafian"-style, as "midgets trying to find a role in the world," would continue to be attacked by suicide bombers. "We will hear similar good news in the coming days," he said, adding that the four thousand mujahideen were from "Saudi Arabia and other countries."

"The flow of these Arabs has begun and people are eager to play their role in a pan-Arab battle to confront the enemies of Islam and their stooges. If American B-52s can kill five hundred people, our human bombs will kill five thousand!" Ramadan declared.

When asked by reporters if bin Laden was involved in sending mujahideen, Yasin said, "We encourage anyone who stands up to aggression."

Although I doubt that bin Laden had direct ties to Saddam Hussein, the Saudi militant had publicly adopted the Iraqi cause about six weeks before the first bombs fell on Baghdad. Bin Laden, never a supporter of Saddam Hussein, had released an audio cassette to al-Jazeera in February in which he called on Muslims around the world to travel to Iraq to fight a jihad against the Americans. Bin Laden said it was a Muslim duty to defend Iraq from the Americans and Zionists, even though he described Iraq as ruled by "socialists," who for bin Laden were tantamount to godless infidels.

Bin Laden spoke before the war like a seasoned general, giving Iraqis tactical advice after having battled the Americans in Afghanistan and lived to fight another day.

"We are with you and we will fight in the name of God," bin Laden said, addressing the Iraqi people. "Our brothers, the mujahideen in Iraq, don't be afraid of America's lies about their powers and their military might. We advise you to drag the forces into street fighting. Take them into farms, into cities, and fight them there."

Although the speech proves Saddam and Osama were bound by a shared hatred of the United States, I don't believe it was evidence of a direct connection between the two men.

Saddam Hussein simply didn't have anything to gain by forging an alliance with bin Laden; it wasn't worth the risk. Saddam was first and foremost a dictator, concerned primarily with maintaining his rule, not changing the world. Although Saddam peppered his speeches with verses from the Koran and was in the process of building several huge mosques in Baghdad when the war started, his desire for power superseded any moral or religious beliefs he had. Saddam crushed religious fundamentalists in Iraq and would never have shared power with bin Laden the way the Taliban had done in Afghanistan, nor would he have allowed such a dangerous, volatile and provocative loose cannon like al-Qaeda to operate in his country. It would have taken control out of Saddam's hands. I also highly doubt Saddam would have ever considered handing bin Laden weapons of mass destruction to attack the United States or Israel—a threat suggested by the Bush administration—because it would have been tantamount to signing over Iraq's fate to bin Laden. I think bin Laden's offer of support, however, became much more appealing to the Iraqi leadership during the final days of the war and during the period of post-war resistance.

This is not to say that President Saddam Hussein had any aversion to making alliances with terrorists. Saddam, in fact, sheltered and employed the Palestinian terrorists Mohammed al-Abbas (Abu al-Abbas) and the notorious Sabri al-Banna, better known as Abu Nidal. Iraq's symbiotic, financial and mercenary relationships with the two Palestinian militants, however, were significantly different from any type of coalition he could have formed with al-Qaeda.

I met Abu Abbas in Baghdad shortly before the war at the headquarters of his group, the Palestinian Liberation Front (PLF). The office was a spacious villa guarded by three men with assault rifles and surrounded by a high cement wall. Parked in the villa's courtyard was a high-end BMW and a Land Rover, evidence that Abu Abbas—in Iraq since 1994— had grown rich in his new home, mainly from the oil smuggling business he was involved in with Saddam's son Uday.

Abu Abbas, a strong man with broad shoulders, a thick mustache and a deep voice, greeted me in his office with a firm handshake. After a coffee and chitchat about the impending war—which he thought was unavoidable—Abu Abbas proudly told me that he was mainly responsible for channeling money from Iraq to the families of Palestinian suicide bombers in the West Bank and Gaza Strip. The money came from Saddam. It was his way of supporting the intifada. Relatives of suicide bombers were given checks for between $10,000 and $25,000, according to Abu Abbas's representative in the Palestinian territories, Rakad Salim, whom I'd interviewed in Ramallah shortly before he was arrested by Israeli forces in October 2002.

In Baghdad, Abu Abbas seemed somewhat nervous about the approaching war despite his calm, sturdy demeanor. He asked me several times if I thought the war was really coming and how far I thought the United States was prepared to go.

Abu Abbas had good reason to worry. He was wanted by Italian authorities for the 1985 hijacking of the Italian cruise ship the *Achille Lauro* and the murder of Leon Klinghoffer, a sixty-nine-year-old wheelchair-bound Jewish-American passenger. Abu Abbas told me his men had never intended to hijack the *Achille Lauro*, but planned to use weapons they'd smuggled on board to carry out an attack at the Israeli port of Haifa. Abu Abbas said his men had only commandeered the cruise ship after they were discovered by the ship's security while at sea.

Abu Abbas was ultimately arrested shortly after the fall of Baghdad. He'd tried to flee to Syria, but was turned away at the border and later picked up near Baghdad by US special forces.

The fact that Abu Abbas had operated so openly in a society as controlled as Iraq's is evidence that Saddam Hussein didn't consider him a threat. Saddam's relationship with Abu Nidal, a man whom British Middle East expert and author Patrick Seale described as "a gun for hire," was significantly different.

Abu Nidal had a long history with Iraq. He was based in Baghdad in the mid-1970s when Yasser Arafat's *Fatah* movement expelled him for being too radical and for allegedly plotting to murder his Palestinian opponents. Saddam Hussein found the then stranded and enraged Abu Nidal (an Arabic *nom de guerre* that means "father of resistance") to be a useful operative to settle scores with Iraq's longtime rival Syria. Saddam, however, expelled Abu Nidal from the country in 1983 to win US support for Iraq's war with Iran. Abu Nidal moved to

Syria and then to Libya, offering his services as a world-class hit man. Before bin Laden, Abu Nidal had been the world's most wanted man, credited with carrying out more than ninety terrorist attacks that killed more than three hundred people. He specialized in highly organized assaults, which he carried out in twenty foreign nations, including attacks at the Rome and Vienna airports in 1985. Abu Nidal was known for his extensive planning, and he was known to have buried weapons in public parks in foreign capitals so they'd be available at a moment's notice.

By the 1990s, however, Abu Nidal had dropped out of the international scene. He was suffering from leukemia and, after allegedly receiving treatment in Cairo in 1997, settled back in Baghdad. His interests are said to have shifted to the arms trade—a longtime source of income—and extorting protection money from Gulf nations. It's unclear why Saddam allowed Abu Nidal to return to Iraq. It's speculated that it was because of business ties with Saddam's son Uday, although I haven't seen convincing evidence. Saddam's loyalties to Abu Nidal, however, were obviously not too deep, because he had the Palestinian militant killed in August 2002.

A Palestinian journalist first reported in Ramallah that Abu Nidal had been shot dead in a Baghdad apartment by Saddam's security forces. Iraqi officials initially said Abu Nidal had barricaded himself in the bathroom and shot himself rather than be arrested. Witnesses who saw Abu Nidal's body, however, said he'd been shot several times, ruling out suicide.

Abu Abbas told me he believed Saddam had Abu Nidal killed because the Palestinian militant had formed an alliance with Iraq's enemy Kuwait. The exact reason may never be known. I believe Saddam had Abu Nidal eliminated because he'd become too much of a liability. During the buildup to the war, officials in Washington had pointed to Abu Nidal's presence in Iraq as evidence that Saddam was harboring terrorists. Just as Saddam expelled Abu Nidal in the 1980s to win the United States' favor, I think he hoped to score points this time by removing Abu Nidal once and for all; it was his way of avoiding the war, the opposite impulse of striking up a relationship with someone as provocative as America's number-one enemy, Osama bin Laden.

The fact remains, however, that bin Laden did call for a jihad in defense of Saddam Hussein's Iraq. I believe it was bin Laden's way of maintaining relevance after the attacks against the World Trade Center and the Pentagon. By associating his name with the conflict in Iraq, bin Laden was trying to latch on to the next hot thing. If Americans were going to be killed in large numbers in Iraq, bin Laden wanted to be part of it. Bin Laden would also try to get in on the act after the war.

I met several Arab mujahideen at the Palestine Hotel during the final days of the war, and I found them to be like other respondents to calls for jihad I'd met in Yemen and Egypt. The men were young, idealistic, disgruntled religious zealots who'd answered the call to jihad, only to be disillusioned by what they found.

In Yemen in 2002, I met about a dozen men who'd fought

in Afghanistan alongside the Taliban. They were from the city of Ta'izz, a stronghold of the Islamic Islah (reform) party, and the remote Hadramout region, bin Laden's ancestral homeland along Yemen's largely unregulated border with Saudi Arabia. The Yemeni mujahideen were rugged, straight-talking, rural villagers with hard worker's hands, profound Islamic convictions and a firm belief that their religion was under attack by the United States and Jews and that it was their duty to put their terrestrial lives on hold to defend their Muslim brethren wherever they were in danger. These men thought of themselves as reservists in a world Muslim army, willing to be called up at a moment's notice. The men seemed very proud of their sacrifices and repeatedly told me what a hardship it had been to leave their businesses and families behind while they set off to make the ultimate sacrifice for the sake of Islam. I met the men at a house in Sanaa in a meeting arranged by a sympathetic Yemeni politician. The rendezvous had to be secret because, much to the mujahideen's surprise and profound disappointment, the Yemeni government no longer agreed with their mission and had started to hunt them down in collaboration with the FBI, which sent agents to Yemen after the September 11 attacks, and the CIA, which had been helping Yemen's President Ali Abdullah Saleh interrogate terrorist suspects. I found the Yemeni war veterans, with wizened faces and traditional curved daggers around their brightly colored gold and silver embroidered belts, to be utterly depressed and furious at their government. They'd returned home after fighting against the Americans in Afghanistan only to be scorned. Many had lost friends in battle and had expected to be welcomed home like heroes, greater than veterans of normal wars because they'd been fighting for God. Instead, the men found themselves on the run like petty thieves. They felt especially betrayed because when they'd left for Afghanistan many sectors of Yemeni society— charities, Islamic leaders and most people on the streets—had supported their mission with speeches and money; in fact Saudi money channeled to Yemeni sheikhs had paid for most of their travel expenses. Even the Yemeni government had initially been supportive and only reluctantly joined Washington's crackdown on Arab mujahideen after several lightly veiled threats from the Pentagon that Yemen would be attacked if it failed to do so. Now after so much sacrifice, the hardened fighters were angry fugitives. The men I met in Yemen—who'd never met bin Laden, although they said they respected him— were now ripe to join organizations like al-Qaeda and keep on fighting; they had nothing else to do. Al-Qaeda offered them jobs and, perhaps more important, respect for what they'd fought for and the opportunity to take revenge on both the Arab countries who'd stabbed them in the backs—in their minds abandoning Islam—and the Americans and Israelis for allegedly putting them up to the betrayal.

It's not a completely new phenomenon. I found the same attitudes in Cairo in 1999 when I met a group of Egyptians who'd traveled to Afghanistan and fought against the Soviet Union in the 1980s. At the time, their decision to go to war in Afghanistan had similarly been considered a noble sacrifice for Islam. But when they returned to Egypt, many were arrested by the suspicious Egyptian government and put on trial by unfair military tribunals, which handed down death sentences after a single hearing.

As Yemen's President Saleh had done under pressure after the September 11 attacks, Egypt's President Mubarak had turned on the Islamists, in his case, after they assassinated his predecessor Anwar Sadat during a parade in October 1981 to mark the 1973 Arab-Israeli war. When I met the Egyptians in 1999 they were still living like criminals under the watchful eye of the Egyptian intelligence services.

Bin Laden's personal history is a similar tale of jihad and betrayal. Bin Laden left a life of luxury to fight what he believed to be a religious war against the godless Soviet Union in Afghanistan. Many powerful Saudis had supported him when he set off, but in April 1994 the Saudi government stripped him of his citizenship and branded him an outlaw. Bin Laden—who acquaintances say is charismatic, calm, polite, soft-spoken and gregarious—decided to keep on fighting and has never stopped, first forming in 1998 the World Islamic Front for Jihad against Jews and Crusaders and eventually al-Qaeda ("the base"), a union of embittered Arab veterans of "holy wars" in Afghanistan (twice), Albania, Bosnia, Chechnya, Dagestan and, most recently, Iraq. He's given purpose to thousands of mujahideen who have no home to return to when the fighting ends.

In 1989, bin Laden was joined by the skilled tactician Ayman al-Zawahiri, an Egyptian physician who would become his trusted deputy and heir apparent. Al-Zawahiri, who has used the code names Abu Mohammed and Abu Fatima, has been described as a private, intelligent and vindictive person. After serving three years in an Egyptian jail for suspected involvement in the assassination of President Sadat, al-Zawahiri traveled to Afghanistan in 1984 to support the mujahideen's medical personnel. After the war, al-Zawahiri moved to Europe, residing in Switzerland and Denmark, according to Egyptian security officials. Al-Zawahiri supposedly carries Egyptian, French, Swiss and Dutch passports, although Switzerland denies he was ever issued one of its passports. Egyptian officials say his French and Swiss passports are under the name Amin Othman and that his Dutch passport, number 513116, is in the name Sami Mahmoud.

Until the September 11 attacks, rhetoric from men like al-Zawahiri about fighting the enemies of Islam wasn't taken very seriously. Now, Washington is presumably reexamining statements from al-Zawahiri that it may previously have considered bluster, including his threat in 1999 to use chemical and biological weapons against the United States and Israel.

At the Palestine Hotel, the Arab volunteers I met had decided to turn themselves in, oddly enough to journalists, thinking we somehow had the power to protect them from US troops. Among them was a Yemeni—a jittery boy of about nineteen—who was worried the Americans would arrest him and send him to Guantanamo Bay. I rushed off to find my DV camera to interview him, but by the time I returned he'd disappeared. Instead I found another group of Lebanese mujahideen huddled by the hotel's entrance. They claimed to be from Hezbollah, a Shiite militant group supported by Iran and Syria and classified by the State Department as an international terrorist organization. Hezbollah had fought Israel in Lebanon from 1982 until Israeli Prime Minister Ehud Barak ended Israel's occupation of southern Lebanon in May 2000. Hezbollah is also credited throughout the Arab world with the defeat of the Israeli army in Lebanon and has earned tremendous popular respect, achieving an almost mythical status. The group has become the model for, and the trainers of, Muslim militants around the world, sending experts in bomb making to the Palestinian territories, among other hot spots.

The men I saw at the Palestine were wearing dirty white T-shirts covered in sweat stains. One man had a bloody bandage around his head. Another had blood-stained gauze wrapped around his knee. They all looked exhausted. I saw them talking to a Lebanese television correspondent and walked over to eavesdrop. The men said they'd been fighting alongside the *fedayeen* and had come to Baghdad looking for safe passage back to Lebanon. I grabbed my turn with them when the Lebanese reporter left to find his camera crew. The fighters told me they'd traveled to Iraq on a bus from Syria not to defend Saddam Hussein, but out of concern that Syria would be America's next target if Iraq fell. After the war, I was told that most of the Arab mujahideen were Syrians.

The Lebanese fighters said they hated Saddam for killing fellow Shiite Muslims, but had put their differences aside for the greater good of Syria and Islam. I have my doubts, however, that they were really Hezbollah fighters. Hezbollah strikes me as too cautious and centrally controlled to allow a few ragtag fighters to cross the border and fight for Iraq. I think these young men were probably affiliated with Hezbollah, but perhaps something less than full members. I'd met Hezbollah before in Lebanon and knew them to be a highly disciplined and organized group, so much that they still run neighborhoods in Beirut and most of southern Lebanon. Hezbollah even has its own television station—Al-Manar— the incendiary network responsible for planting the prevailing rumor in the Arab world that Jews working at the World Trade Center were given prior notice to the September 11 attacks.

When I first arrived in Lebanon in 2002 I made contact with Hezbollah's headquarters, a bustling apartment in southern Beirut. I'd met the press liaison, who photocopied my passport and telephoned his counterpart in the South and organized a visit for me of towns along the Israeli border under Hezbollah's unofficial control.

I was under the impression that I'd made strong inroads with the group when I returned to Beirut after my tour of the South. I returned to Hezbollah's headquarters and asked the press contact for an interview with one of the group's political leaders, a member of the Lebanese parliament. The press attaché, his face and head marred with purple scars (he'd previously been a fighter), set the appointment for later that afternoon. With several hours before my meeting I decided to finish a feature I'd been working on about life in the Arab world during Ramadan, the Islamic holy month in which Muslims fast all day and feast at night. It's a unique time in the Muslim world with nightly festive dinner meals, called *iftars*, in which guests are often treated to dried dates and heaping plates of grilled lamb on rice, often followed by honey-coated desserts. I left Hezbollah's office, telling the press contact that I'd be back for the meeting, and ventured out with a driver I knew into the Shiite Muslim neighborhood.

I was in a bakery that specialized in flat, pancake-like cookies filled with sweet cheese and raisins (a Ramadan specialty) when a man who looked to be in his early twenties walked in and lingered in the doorway, staring at me.

"Hey," he called to me. "There are some people in the neighborhood who want to talk to you."

"Who are you?" I asked him, thinking little of his presence.

"There are people who want to meet you," was all he replied.

"Look, I'm a journalist doing a story on Ramadan, do you want to be interviewed?" I asked.

He was silent.

"I think we should go," I told my driver, assuming we'd somehow hit a nerve in this poor urban neighborhood.

We walked out of the store and headed back to our car, parked a few blocks away. When we reached the corner, a Range Rover with tinted windows accelerated in front of us and screeched to a halt. The Jeep's four doors opened simultaneously and five men descended from the vehicle. Two men were carrying AK-47s at their sides.

"Get in the car," one of the men ordered me. He had a closely cropped beard and a lean and muscular physique.

"Hey, I'm just here doing a story about Ramadan," I said in Arabic. "What's the problem?"

"Get in the car," he repeated. I instinctively backed away from the Jeep until I had my back—both literally and metaphorically—against a wall. The men made a semicircle around the driver and me. I slipped out of their ring of force and ran up to a man selling fruit from a cart on the street corner.

"Did you hear me talking about Ramadan?" I asked him, hoping he'd vouch for me.

"I swear to God, I don't know," he said in a nervous, stumbling voice.

"Don't talk to him," the man with the beard warned. The group had shifted and was now completely encircling me.

"Don't get in the car," the driver whispered to me, as if I wasn't thinking the same thing. I considered running, but to where? I thought they'd shoot me if I ran.

"You guys are from the resistance, right?" I asked, referring to Hezbollah as the Lebanese call it. "That's fine. Let's just walk to your office. They know me there. We can clear up this misunderstanding in a second." I faked optimism in my voice, as if this was just a minor quibble.

The man with the close-cropped beard grabbed me roughly by the upper arm. He was unnecessarily violent, pinching my skin in his fingers and squishing the muscle in his hand. "Don't make a scene, just get in the car!" he grumbled in my ear. Another one of the men grabbed my other arm so tightly his grip left four deep bruises where his fingers had been. The two brutes threw me through an open car door like a sack of flour. They tossed the driver in too. The rest of the Hezbollah squad jumped in the Range Rover as it was pulling away, slamming shut the doors. My breathing was short as I sat sandwiched between the two men with assault rifles. "Look," I repeated, "you guys are from the resistance, right?" One of the more innocent-faced gunmen nodded in acknowledgment. It was evidently protocol not to speak to me because the vehicle was deadly silent. I slowly pulled a mobile phone from my pocket, raising it in the air, making an obvious display that I wasn't brandishing a weapon. "I'll call your office and tell them what has happened, okay? They can vouch for me that I'm just a journalist." I started dialing when one of the men karate-chopped my hand, sending the phone flying.

"Okay, no calls," I said. "Look, let's just drive to the office," I begged, but within minutes we whizzed past Hez-bollah's headquarters, taking left and right turns down alleys and streets that were completely unfamiliar to me. After what was probably only a ten-minute drive—it seemed like we were heading all the way to Syria—the Jeep pulled up to a gated residential compound of sterile, tan, nondescript 1980s-Mediterranean–style apartment buildings.

A guard pushed a button to roll back a green sliding metal gate, revealing a parking lot in the center of the compound.

One man who'd squeezed my arm wrenched the bag I'd been carrying away from me. I didn't know why they were being so aggressive. I'd been arrested many times in Egypt, mostly for videotaping without a permit. Egypt, home of the most noisome bureaucracy I know, has strict rules about taking pictures without permission from the Information Ministry, which of course is not easy to obtain. But every time I was taken in by police in Cairo it had been the same routine: They yelled at me for a few minutes, then served tea, asked me stupid questions about Jewish conspiracies, and finally let me go after making me promise I'd come back to visit. This was completely different. I was scared for my life.

The Hezbollah guard started digging through my bag, pulling out my recording equipment and passport. Luckily, my other passport, the one with Israeli stamps, I'd left hidden in my room at the Commodore Hotel.

"Go inside," a man said as he opened my car door.

"What?" I asked. "Inside where?"

"Are you Egyptian?" he asked.

"No, I'm an American," I said. I couldn't bluff. He already had my passport.

He didn't seem fazed that I was an American, though, and repeated his order to get inside, pointing to one of the apartment buildings.

"Why can't I just stay here while you do whatever it is you have to do? Check on me, whatever," I suggested. I wanted to stay in the courtyard. At least I could see the sky, which made me feel freer.

"Do you have anything in your wallet?" the man who'd opened the door asked me. I looked at him like he was a criminal, trying to shame him with a shocked expression. "You're supposed to be a political activist and an Islamist, not a petty thief," I tried to make my look say. I knew he wasn't going to steal from me, Hezbollah wouldn't have done that, but I didn't want him rifling through my wallet—and it was lucky for me that he didn't.

The bully with the short beard grabbed me again and pushed me into the building. I was walking slowly up the raw-concrete staircase. One of the men was pushing me from behind so I would climb faster. Other men with assault rifles slung over their shoulders passed me on their way out of the building. When we reached the third floor, I was led into an apartment. The front room had three cells in it with prison-style metal doors that had slats in them for air. Each of the heavy doors had a sliding hatch the size of a mail slot, evidently used to pass food or water to the prisoner. Sliding metal bolts locked the doors from the outside. Two men pushed me inside one of the cells and I heard the bolt clank into place with the distinctive sound of metal on metal. The cell was so tiny I could touch both walls with my outstretched arms. It was smaller than most closets. There were no windows. It was completely dark.

I was in the unfortunate position of knowing what Hezbollah had done to hostages it had taken in the past. The group had kept the Associated Press journalist Terry Anderson hostage for six years and killed three hostages in 1986 in retaliation for the US bombing of Libya and Israeli attacks against the Palestine Liberation Organization (PLO).

Then it hit me like a lightning bolt that I had an Israeli press ID in my wallet. That's when I really got scared. It had been a stupid oversight. I was angry with myself and frightened. I'd purposely left my other passport at the hotel, but forgotten to leave my Israeli press ID behind. The press card, the size of a credit card, had my name typed on it in English and Hebrew and a picture of me, half covered with a gold seal shaped like a menorah. I took out my wallet and managed to identify the ID card in the almost total blackness of the cell by holding it right up to my face. The card was printed on hard plastic. There was no way I could have eaten it. I thought about ditching it in the cell, but then realized the guards would search it once they'd taken me out. I decided I had to hide it on my body. I hoped that if they never found the ID they wouldn't strip-search me. I was still fairly confident that my captors would eventually call the Hezbollah office and that the press liaison would vouch for me. But if these guards discovered the Israeli ID card, which I hadn't told the press representative about, it would be a completely different story. I imagined a conversation between my captors and the Hezbollah press officer.

"We found an American named Richard Engel, do you know him?" I pictured the toughest guy asking.

"Yeah, he was here earlier," the press guy would say.

"We also found on him an Israeli identity card."

"Really?

"Yeah, really."

"Well, I don't know anything about that. See who he is."

Then the beatings would have started, and who knows what else.

I was also eavesdropping on the guards and heard them say, "What if this guy is like that Jew captured in Afghanistan?" They were referring to Daniel Pearl, the *Wall Street Journal* reporter kidnapped and killed by Muslim fundamentalists in Pakistan in January 2002.

I started chewing up the Israeli ID card, tearing it apart in my teeth. I wanted to break the card into small pieces and hide it in my sock between my toes. I pulled at the plastic with my teeth, slicing my gums, which started bleeding. About four hours later—it seemed like an eternity—the door slid open. The man with the close-cropped beard said, "You can go. You can go ahead and finish your story and if anyone stops you, tell them that you've been with the *ihwan* (brothers) from security."

I told him that I had enough material for my story and would be on my way, thank you very much.

I called the Hezbollah press attaché from the car when we were a safe distance out of the neighborhood and asked him what the big idea had been. He didn't apologize, and only said, "You should have told me where you were going."

"This isn't your city," I said, but obviously it was.

My brief history with Hezbollah made me especially interested in what the Lebanese mujahideen who'd limped to the Pales-tine to surrender had to say. If they were indeed Hezbollah, it would have taken a lot to push them to give up. I knew the war had been getting more intense over the last few days, but I hadn't seen the worst of it. Since the sandstorm, I'd heard the constant thud of bombings around the perimeter of Baghdad, but had no idea what was being destroyed. It was too far away for me to see and the reporters embedded with the US military were still too far south. The bombings were happening in a blind spot, a part of the war I don't think has been recorded. In my opinion, it was during these persistent off-camera raids that many of the Iraqi casualties took place. The Pentagon said at the time that it was eliminating Republican Guards stationed around the edges of Baghdad. Analysts said this was a necessary step before a full-scale invasion of the city, the moment I feared most. Although there's no clear number of the Iraqi soldiers killed during the entire war, Uday al-Ta'e, whom I met with in Baghdad in July, told me he estimated about fifteen thousand members of the Iraqi military were killed in the war, although I'm sure the exact number will be debated for years to come.

The young Lebanese fighters said thousands of Iraqis and other Arab fighters like them had been killed. It was obvious from their tired voices, drooping eyes and exhausted postures, let alone their bloody bandages and filthy, sweat-stained clothing, that these young men had seen horrifying battles. They said they'd been fighting alongside the *fedayeen* about twenty miles south of Baghdad. They described with awe how the American planes dropped bombs on them at night, using their hands to

simulate the planes soaring overhead, turning their camp into
an inferno of scorched earth and flying shrapnel. They'd fled
the area and hitchhiked to Baghdad to find a way home.

There was only one reporter I know of who actually saw
some of this fighting firsthand: my neighbor at the Palestine,
Efi Pentaraki from Greece's Star Channel. Her minder,
Mohammed, was different from all the other press center
officials. He was the complete opposite of Abu Annas, being
young, hyperactive and extremely helpful. He was always tin-
kering in Efi's room, for example, and rewired her lights to
make them brighter. He even built a platform on her balcony
out of cardboard for her satellite phone to give it better
reception. Mohammed openly told Efi that he worked for
Iraqi intelligence and, in a somewhat macho way, took it
upon himself to be her personal bodyguard. He always carried a pistol, which he would leave on her dressing table
whenever he came into the room. Mohammed—who couldn't
focus on a single topic for long and was scatterbrained but
obviously smart—took Efi to places no other reporters had
access to or dared to go by themselves, including the edge of
Baghdad during the most intense bombing. She told me she
saw thousands of Republican Guards packed into private
homes around the edges of the city. The soldiers were sitting
around, she said, evidently waiting for the Americans to
enter.

While Efi had been out reporting, a missile struck a telephone exchange next to her in broad daylight. Luckily, she

wasn't killed, or even injured. She even kept filming during the raid with her mini-DV camera. Efi's crew had left Iraq fearing for their safety, leaving her alone. On the tape, Mohammed the minder, in an incredible act of bravery, ran into the building and started digging for survivors. Efi ran in after him along with Patrick Baz, a superb photographer from the French News Agency AFP. Together, the three of them pulled from the rubble an old man, whose head was bleeding profusely. That night, Uday al-Ta'e brought Mohammed, Patrick and Efi a cake and several bottles of Pepsi and 7 UP to acknowledge their bravery. Efi told me Mohammed had been crying on the drive back to Baghdad. It was a peculiar time of mixed emotions, odd friendships, bizarre alliances and solidarity among everyone in the battle zone, friend and foe alike.

The pounding around Baghdad was also for me a constant reminder that the American war machine was heading my way. I still worried Baghdad would erupt when US tanks rolled down Saadoon Street and wasn't satisfied with my flimsy network of safe houses. I knew I couldn't count on Zafar to be at the hotel I'd booked him and had written him off as an option. I hadn't been back to re-visit my pharmacist. I did make contact, however, with a Sudanese television crew that, amazingly, had managed to stay below the Information Ministry's radar. Oddly, they weren't staying at the Palestine Hotel, nor did they have government minders. I guess the Iraqis weren't concerned about what Sudanese television broadcast. The Sudanese team was staying in an apartment one block away from the Palestine, and I assumed my best bet in a pinch would be to get to them. I calculated it would take me between ten and fifteen minutes to run down the fourteen flights of stairs from my room to the ground floor, sprint one block and reach their apartment. It was a decent option.

I started seriously reconsidering my options, however, after *Newsday* reporter Matthew "Matt" McAllester went missing, along with photographers Moises Saman, Molly Bingham and Johan Spanner. Matt, a friend I'd worked with in the West Bank, had last been seen on March 24 when he'd been working on a story. One of Matt's close friends, Larry Kaplow from the Cox group of newspapers, took it especially hard. In a completely selfless act, Larry made it his personal mission to find out what happened to Matt and the other reporters. Larry knew that by digging into their disappearance—stirring the pot—he was antagonizing the local officials, whom we were all confident had arrested Matt and the other reporters. Larry hounded me and every other foreign reporter affiliated with a major media outlet to see if we could find out any information, and if possible, pressure the Iraqis. If I ever go missing in a war zone, I hope Larry is around to help me. The reporters in Baghdad had finally become a tight group. We were defending one another. It made me proud.

I was especially nervous for Matt because, like me, he'd been based in Jerusalem before coming to Iraq. I also empathized with Matt because he'd entered Iraq on a sketchy visa linked to the human shields.

Matt and the other reporters were eventually released unharmed after a harrowing week in Abu Greib, one of the worst prisons in the Middle East and probably the world. He'd been accused of being a spy, but was let go. I took it as a warning.

CHAPTER SEVEN

April 3

The power just went out in Baghdad. I've never seen such beautiful stars. At first, I thought the dots in the sky—in space—were high-altitude aircraft; some in fact might have been. I tried to memorize the positions of the lights to see if they moved. I am now writing by candlelight and one lamp. I have my generator running on the balcony, which I'm using to charge everything I can get my hands on: sat phone, dv camera, batteries, etc.

I was shocked a few minutes ago at how much power my little hot water heater sucks. I made dinner (Chinese noodles again) and when I plugged the water heater into the generator, it went into overdrive.

Mohammed, Efi the Greek's fixer/minder/slightly insane friend is coming over in a few minutes to help me steal power from the one emergency light still on in my room. He's going to rip the light off the wall, cut open the wire and run half of it into an extension cord. It's a very clever solution. He already did it in Efi's room.

For some odd reason I'm excited and in a good mood. I'm jazzed up and have had the song "The Rivers of Babylon" stuck in my head all day long. I must learn the words to the rest of the song when I get out of this because now I only know the first line.

I was high on adrenaline and had switched into my crisis mode. "Get organized! Get ready!" I told myself, like a mantra. In some peculiar way I was enjoying it. I filled the bathtub, along with several large plastic jugs, with water. For the past week, I'd bought a 5-liter jerrican every day to fill with tap water. I'd need lots of water to wash myself and flush the toilet, which stopped running as soon as the power went.

I hunted for my little flashlight, concerned the emergency light would go out at any moment. I also made sure I could find my sweaty bundle of money, which I always wore around my ankle in a spandex sleeve. It had become black and rancid, but I loved it anyway. It was my secret weapon, my escape money, and I was forever worried I'd lose it.

I wanted to be ready at a moment's notice, which also made sleeping something of an issue. I don't generally sleep with any clothing on, which could potentially have led to somewhat awkward circumstances if the hotel caught fire, was stormed by *fedayeen* or if bepistoled intelligence agents burst into my room in the dead of night. I envisioned myself standing outside the Palestine Hotel naked as a fish, a bed sheet wrapped around me like a swami, redfaced in front of the other reporters. It wouldn't have looked very professional.

After the power went out the mood in Baghdad turned. The war had finally come to town. Restaurants were locked up tight. Streets were virtually empty. No one could any longer pretend the war was going to blow over like a thunderstorm.

I tried to stay outside the hotel as much as possible. I liked the protection that the Palestine seemed to offer, but didn't like that all the Westerners were gathered in a single place. I wanted to stay mobile, and every day slipped out the hotel's back door, avoiding Abu Annas, and spent hours running errands, finding the few open shops in town and talking to people. I didn't stray far from the hotel, but liked the fact that I was in a car. I felt more in control and, as long as I didn't do any filming, I didn't attract too much attention. My meanderings were also helpful because they always gave me material for my reports. Otherwise, I would have had to rely more heavily on the daily briefings from al-Sahaf and other Iraqi ministers.

Al-Sahaf said the Americans were responsible for blacking out Baghdad. It seemed plausible, considering they were doing all the bombing, including dropping one explosive so close to the hotel at dinnertime (penne and tomato sauce, broiled chicken, and stewed zucchini of course) that it sent

me diving to the floor. Al-Sahaf said the American forces—
whom he had recently started calling "desert animals" and
"boa constrictors"—knocked out the power to deliberately
terrorize the Iraqi people, thus proving the US administration's
lie of coming to liberate Iraq. The Pentagon, in typically sug-
gestive yet noncommittal language, said that "it was entirely
possible" that the Iraqis themselves had turned the lights off in
Baghdad. I found this plausible too, suspecting that the Iraqis
might have blacked out the city ahead of the main battle for
the capital, which seemed to be coming any day.

The Iraqis had also realized that unlike the 1991 Gulf
War, this war would be decisive. In fact, the Iraqi propaganda machine oddly dubbed the war the "Decisive Days."
It was Iraq's equivalent to "Operation Iraqi Freedom." I was
surprised to learn that the Iraqis had labeled the war the
Decisive Days because it didn't seem to me to be particularly
optimistic. I would have expected names more like the Battle
of Martyrdom, the Great Jihad, or even Days of Victory. It
was as if, deep down, the Iraqi government knew the war
spelled the end of the Saddam system no matter what the
outcome.

I subsequently learned after the war from a senior US military official involved in the reconstruction of Iraq that it was
in fact the Americans who blacked out Baghdad. The official
said the US bombing campaign had been selective because the
military always knew it would eventually have to restore
power. But military planners didn't anticipate the damage the
looters would inflict after the city fell.

April 4

It's hot: 90 degrees or more. There's a lot of activity in the
streets. It may all be starting. I think we have a few more days.
I went to the market today. There are now stalls set up selling
batteries, water jugs and some food. It's mostly emergency
supplies. I was surprised to see people out walking in the
market. I think when people don't know what to do, and
receive no direction from their government, they just do what
they always do.

There were many blank looks on people's faces. Baghdad
is now a city without a life. It is like a city modeled after one
of Alberto Giacometti's sculptures. I think the lack of clear
action is a result of the "Big Brother" culture here. Today's
newspaper headline was typical of the prevailing message:
"The Leader Says Victory Is Assured And In Our Hands!"
With information like that, it's no wonder why people freeze.

I slept through *Nightline* last night. I was just wiped out.
I couldn't get up. I'm running on almost no sleep. The time
has also changed, further complicating my feed times. I hope
the editors aren't too pissed.

I think there will be heavy bombings around the edges
of the city over the next three to four days and then the big
push.

Streams of buses had started heading out of the city again.
Many families had already abandoned Baghdad for the countryside at the start of the war, often leaving a single male relative or two to guard the family home or business. Now, those
last hangers-on were fleeing too.

Food was rapidly becoming scarce. Ali couldn't find the cheese and bread we'd been having for breakfast each day. Bakeries were shut and fruit and vegetable markets were empty. We started tapping into my reserves of crackers, tuna fish, Chinese noodles and candy bars.

The government officials and minders also were no longer as calm and cocky as before. Uday al-Ta'e—who would become docile and sweet after the war—had become a furious tyrant, ordering journalists to leave Iraq (at considerable risk, considering the road to Jordan was under attack) for the most minor infractions; I even saw him rip a camera from a German correspondent's hands because he'd gone out filming without his minder. Uday had also essentially locked up about ten journalists who'd amazingly, and somewhat foolishly, driven to Baghdad from Kuwait, pulling up in front of the Palestine Hotel in their dust-covered Land Rovers without a prior invitation. Uday confined the new arrivals—almost all of them Italian newspaper reporters—to rooms in the Palestine. They were not allowed to leave, file stories or use other journalists' satellite telephones. If they broke the rules, they'd been told, they would be arrested, one of them told me. The new arrivals were an odd addition to our little knot of reporters at the Palestine and spent most of the final days of the war smoking cigarettes and chatting loudly together in the coffee shop, eventually teaching the manager how to make a decent espresso, which was a welcome Italian contribution to the war effort.

After the war, Uday told me that he'd fought to allow the walk-ins to stay at the Palestine. The intelligence service, Uday said, had wanted to imprison them. There were certainly power struggles between the press center officials—who more or less understood what journalists did for a living—and the intelligence service, who considered us all spies. But it's difficult to know how hard Uday really fought for us because, like so many Iraqis, he started rewriting his personal history after the war.

After the fall of Baghdad, anyone affiliated with the Saddam system—officials, businessmen or even academics who benefited from positions of power—became overnight partisans. Interviewing people in Baghdad after the war, it seemed no one ever supported Saddam, much the same way I assume it was hard to find a Nazi sympathizer in US-occupied Berlin in 1950. There were thousands of people who benefited from Saddam's reign of fear, obtaining powerful or lucrative contracts, which—drunk with the impunity and protection only dictatorships can provide—they more often than not abused. Grassroots militias and vigilantes would begin settling decades' worth of old scores shortly after the fall of Baghdad, gunning down former business leaders, professors and Baath party officials in their homes and on the streets.

The blackout, and the final exodus from Baghdad it prompted, also opened the door to thieves. Opportunistic Iraqis—almost always young men dressed in shabby track suits—also started approaching the Palestine Hotel, hunting for unattended bags or equipment. I watched them stalk the lawn in front of the hotel, at first mingling with the surrendering Arab fighters—some of whom had set up a tent on the grass as they waited for safe passage home—before circling the grounds, searching for something to pilfer. Ismail noticed the thieves too, and had his chief Iraqi engineer start carrying a gun, which I have no doubt he would have used.

The situation in Baghdad had become unpredictable, and was developing very quickly.

April 4

This war seems to have turned a corner. People have been fleeing the area about the airport. Paul Wood from the BBC was in a hospital in the area when suddenly his minder told him that they had to leave. Later, the minder told Paul that there had been fedayeen in the building looking for American and British journalists to kill. Not good. Not good at all. I'm not sure what to expect. I predict some heavy bombings over the next 3–4 days and then for the US troops to open up a tunnel for Baghdadis to escape through. It's easier to let people escape than to fight them. It will be chaos. There will be suicide attacks. I won't go through that tunnel if it's opened, I don't think. Perhaps I should? We'll see then.

I hardly notice the bombs anymore unless they are very close. They are falling all the time, day and night. It's almost like rain, a constant drizzle with occasional downpours; I don't want to get wet.

I had Chinese noodles (seafood flavor) again for dinner tonight. At least I'm getting exercise, climbing 14 flights of stairs 3–4–5 times a day.

The battle for the Baghdad airport was one of the most confusing episodes of the war, and one that still remains shrouded in mystery. Iraqis insist that the fighting was intense and that the Americans failed to capture the airport during their initial assault. At the time, al-Sahaf also ominously promised that Iraqi forces would use "nonconventional" attacks at the airport, which he said would inflict huge American casualties. The initial assumption was that he was threatening to use the biological or chemical weapons Iraq had allegedly been stockpiling. Al-Sahaf coyly refused to confirm or deny Iraq's intentions, only saying that "the world will soon see." A consummate showman, al-Sahaf added melodrama to his bluster by appealing directly to American soldiers to surrender to Iraqi forces or face "a certain death at the airport." He also called on American families to intervene for the sake of their sons' lives. A few hours after al-Sahaf's threat, American reporters embedded with the military were filing stories from the airport runway.

The battle for the airport was certainly not the turning point the Iraqis had promised; indeed, there were many Iraqi casualties there. Amid what were at the time conflicting reports, I drove to the airport area to see if I could determine who was actually in control.

The roads were empty as I drove past the burned-out wreckage of about a dozen Iraqi tanks and armored personnel carriers about five miles from the airport. I saw the bodies of two Iraqi men facedown in the street and decided not to go any closer. I went to the nearby al-Yarmouk hospital (the same hospital, I later learned, where fedayeen had wanted to kill reporters), and found it packed with hundreds of wounded men of military age. The place was buzzing and there were throngs of people rushing in and out. In the hospital's morgue I saw what must have been a few hundred bodies in rows on the floor. I had been allowed into the morgue by accident, and was inside of it for only a few seconds. I had simply wandered into the room, looking for someone in charge. Once the hospital staff realized I was a reporter, they quickly shooed me away. I wasn't allowed to go back in and take pictures, which wasn't surprising. The Iraqi government's policy on showing its casualties of war had changed during the course of the conflict. During the initial days of fighting, Iraqi newspapers—especially *Babel*—had printed large color photographs of beheaded Iraqi children, severed limbs and close-ups of men with bullet holes in their skulls. But after about two weeks the images stopped being printed, and the Iraqi media mentioned only American and British casualties, often exaggerating them. The Iraqis had initially wanted to galvanize their people's support and make the American campaign look ferocious, drawing a contrast to the US's promise of a precise war of liberation. The gory pictures, however, only terrified the Iraqi people, triggering surrenders and demoralizing the armed forces and their families, according to a reporter from Iraqi state television, who told me after the war he'd been ordered not to broadcast images of Iraqi losses during the final stages of the fighting. Iraq was trying to make the Americans look like bloodthirsty killers and simultaneously make it seem that the United States wasn't winning the war.

The Iraqi propaganda machine was also sensitive to Arab public opinion. I was visiting Uday al-Ta'e in his makeshift office at the Palestine Hotel when he was yelling at the editor in chief of the Iraqi news agency. The state newswire had just run a story saying that six hundred Lebanese fighters had been "martyred" by the Americans. The report had triggered something of a panic in Lebanon, and the Lebanese government was demanding to know who these 600 of its citizens were and what happened to them.

"Six hundred martyred!" Uday screamed. "It's a disaster in Lebanon! Six hundred! It's a disaster!"

The editor in chief of the Al-Qadissiya newspaper, who was also in the room, had a suggestion: "Reprint the article and make it sixty."

Uday still wasn't satisfied. "Make it six," he ordered, and the editor of the Iraqi news agency ran off to make the change.

After the war, I was told that Iraqi "special guards," a force belonging directly to Saddam Hussein, did most of the fighting at the airport. Rumors that Saddam himself directed the battle from atop a tank still circulate in Baghdad today. The battle at the airport, along with the standoff at Um Kasr in southern Iraq, will go down in Iraq as the two (and only) great moments of Iraqi resistance during the war. True or not, the two battles have become part of the collective history that Iraqis carry in their minds. Many Iraqis also believe that hundreds of Americans were killed at the airport, losses they say the Pentagon hid from the American people by tossing the dead bodies from helicopters into the desert. The commander of US forces in Iraq, Lieutenant General Ricardo Sanchez, has repeatedly dismissed the allegation as utterly impossible, but many Iraqis still believe it.

Three months after the war, over a lunch of lamb cubes, chicken kebabs, hummus and beer, I met a man deeply involved in the post-war resistance. He wasn't a gunman, but was a very wealthy Iraqi businessman and a fervent Saddam loyalist. He was also an admirer of Hitler, a relative of a wanted Iraqi intelligence officer, a hater of Shiite Muslims, and a courier of Saddam's audiocassette recordings to the Arab media. He told me Iraq did in fact have plans for a "nonconventional" attack at the airport, like al-Sahaf had threatened. He said the plan had been to flood the airport with water and then to throw massive electrical cables into the puddles, electrocuting the American troops. He said the flooding had been a success, but that the American onslaught had knocked out the power before the Iraqis could electrify the water.

During the final four days of the war, events were developing so quickly it was hard to understand what was happening. There were initially reports from the Pentagon that US forces had entered the center of Baghdad "and were there to stay." It turned out, however, that forces stationed at the airport (which had become the army's base of operations in Baghdad) had stormed through the city, apparently to test the resistance. The experiment, on April 5, was called a "Thunder Run."

April 5

The US says troops are in the heart of Baghdad. It doesn't feel like it here. I think I was just a bit of a buzz kill on *Good Morning America*. I think people wanted me to say, "Yes I saw the troops storming through the city, rolling over statues of Saddam Hussein, and people were cheering 'with our souls, with our blood we sacrifice for America!'"

Instead, I said I didn't see any troops or any sign of their sweep through the city. First I was told there was a tank division downtown and went looking for it. I found nothing. Now it seems the troops were just driving through town on the way back to the airport to see what would happen: the answer—not much, as far as I can tell.

There had in fact been major fighting, but in another part of the city I couldn't get to. I could only confirm what I was able to see. US Central Command said between two and three thousand Iraqis were killed during this Thunder Run.

I awoke the morning of April 6 to a high-pitched crash. I initially thought another bomb had fallen close to the hotel, this time smashing my glass balcony door. Supine in bed, I looked at the door, shaded by a curtain. It seemed to be intact and I was quietly thankful that I'd covered it in so many layers of tape. I noticed, however, a beam of sunlight shining through a small hole in the curtain. I swung my feet to the floor and pulled back the curtain to see what damage had been done. I was shocked to see a round hole in the middle of the door, which was completely fractured. The broken glass was held in place by the layers of tape, making it look like a spider's web with a hole big enough to put two fingers through in the center. "Someone's shooting at me!" I thought and dropped to the floor, tiny bits of glass digging into my knees. I looked around the room and saw where the bullet had lodged into the ceiling. On my hands and knees, I backed away from the balcony and crawled into the bathroom. I wanted to put another wall between me and the balcony. If I'd been standing instead of flat in bed when the shot was fired, the bullet could very easily have struck me in the head, considering the angle at which it tore through the room. After about five minutes in the bathroom wondering who could be shooting at me, I peered into the room, stood up, pulled on my pants, slipped on my ankle sleeve full of cash and started moving my clothing and equipment to another room I'd been keeping in reserve on the twelfth floor.

I do not think I was targeted in any way; rather, that the gunfire had been random, part of the increasing chaos enveloping Baghdad by the hour. The bombings were also growing more intense. The war was clearly spiraling inward toward the capital.

April 7

US tanks are across the river. I thought they might be coming over to my side. I think there was a collective sigh of despair among the journalists here when it became clear that they were not coming over to this side of the river. I've been willing them over all day long.

There was an ominous sign at the hotel today. A group of fedayeen dressed in black came to the lobby and said that no one should leave. Then, they themselves left and didn't come back.

On the morning the army's Third Infantry Division conquered the western half of Baghdad, I awoke to the sound of an American jet buzzing past the hotel. The howling of the jet was so piercing that I jumped off the mattress and went flat on my belly on the carpet, which, like the rest of my new room, was filthy with dust and oil I'd spilled while moving my generator. I had gotten accustomed to the bombings, but the sound of a fighter soaring by at such close range still filled me with terror. I listened to the planes make a number of passes, each time dropping bombs that exploded seconds later. After about ten minutes spread-eagled on the carpet (I was so tired that I prolonged any moment's rest as long as possible), I inched over to the balcony and, squatting on my heels, peered out across the river. I could see two US Bradley fighting vehicles driving along the western bank of the Tigris in front of the Republican Palace. I filmed them with my DV camera as they rolled back and forth, throwing up clouds of smoke, but stopped after a few minutes, afraid the camera's glass lens would cast a reflection and draw fire. The planes were still passing overhead in a steady stream, turning buildings into white clouds of dust.

The Bradleys—like tanks but armed with a 50-caliber machine gun—were only a few hundred yards away, but I was no safer than I was before. In fact this was the most dangerous phase of the war. Half of Baghdad had fallen to the Americans—the wrong half from my perspective, the half I wasn't in.

I called ABC and asked if the Pentagon bureau had any idea when the Third Infantry Division might head my way. *Nightline*'s Ted Koppel was embedded with the division and had made the commanding general, Buford Blount, into a household name. Couldn't he send a couple of tanks my way? I jokingly suggested. I didn't know how long I could stand the wait.

I was told that the Third Infantry Division had advanced faster than expected. They'd gone out on another Thunder Run and, encountering little resistance, pushed all the way to the center of Baghdad. I was told the forces had had no idea that in such a short amount of time they'd be occupying Saddam's main palace, just across the river from me.

The battle for the eastern side of the Tigris—my side—was a different story altogether. In contrast to the army, the marines fighting in the east were advancing more slowly than expected, having encountered stiffer resistance than they'd anticipated. The marines were still a day or two away. Furthermore, I was told the army wouldn't cross the Tigris until the marines were in position on the opposite bank. The army simply didn't have enough forces to take all of Baghdad, and if they crossed the river too early, they'd spread themselves too thin, risking being cut off from the airport—their main base—also on the western bank. So I was waiting for the marines and filing stories non-stop. I didn't leave the hotel for the next two days. The time I'd feared most had come, and I wondered if I'd made the right decision to stay in Iraq.

On April 8 I witnessed the most awesome display of military might I'd seen since the night of Shock and Awe three nights into the war. That initial assault had been furious and spectacular, but also distant and oddly cinemagraphic. On April 8, however, I saw the kind of war that seemed to me to be more deadly: close combat involving bullets, tanks, attack helicopters and the A-10 Warthog with its terrifying Gatling gun.

April 8 was also the end of the Saddam regime as I knew it. Abu Annas and all the other minders left the Palestine Hotel sometime that morning, never to be seen again. Uday al-Ta'e told me later that he'd simply told them to go home, which they evidently did without hesitation. When I came down to the empty lobby that morning I saw ashtrays on the table the minders had been using full of cigarettes stamped out halfway. Apparently, they'd made a quick exit.

Uday al-Ta'e and al-Sahaf, however, stayed at the Palestine until the last moment, although it was becoming clear that they were cut off from their superiors and the front lines. Al-Sahaf also appeared to have been cut off from reality when he made his famous statement that day on the Palestine's roof that American troops—whom we had all seen across the river— were still "hundreds of miles from Baghdad," unable to fight "because they're busy committing suicide on the banks of the Tigris out of desperation at their military failure!"

It was also on April 8 that one of the Third Infantry Division's tanks fired on the Palestine Hotel, killing the two cameramen. A subsequent inquiry acquitted the tank crew and its commander of any wrongdoing, arguing that appropriate force had been used. I don't agree, and believe the decision to fire at the hotel was taken too quickly. The Palestine Hotel was on the Pentagon's list of protected sites in Baghdad, and the hotel was also too far away from the tank—approximately one mile—to have posed any danger to it. A gunman armed with an assault rifle or even RPG wouldn't have been able to shoot at the tank with any accuracy from that distance. Furthermore, if the tank crew believed a suspicious-looking camera was directing fire at it, which was what was ultimately argued (the army's story has changed several times), the tank commander still should have known—as nearly all of the world did—that the Palestine was full of reporters with television cameras.

That night the mood among reporters was both somber and angry as we held our candlelight vigil, spoiled for me by a lone Iraqi protester.

I was running in front of the Palestine Hotel on April 9—the day the rest of Baghdad fell to the American forces—trying to take cover from snipers I believed had taken position in a building across the street, when I saw the tanks roll up in front of the mosque that had been my backdrop for much of the war. The marines had finally arrived! I turned on my heel, sprinted up the stairs to the live-position on the first floor balcony of the Palestine and watched the marines fan out from their vehicles, guns ready. They were being very cautious, moving slowly and meticulously. They didn't seem nervous, but were clearly taking precautions. Within about a quarter of an hour of the marines' arrival, a crowd of curious Iraqis cautiously approached them. Some of the Iraqis at the front of the crowd were bare-chested, and were waving their white undershirts to signal that they didn't mean harm. It was this group of about two hundred people who started pulling down Saddam's statue, providing one of the most enduring images of the war. A group of men (later joined by about a dozen women) tied a thick rope around Saddam's neck like a noose and tugged but failed to budge the mammoth statue—one of many of Saddam with his right arm extended in a gesture of magnanimity. A hulking man from the crowd had brought a sledgehammer and started swinging away at the statue's cement base, chipping it but doing little real damage. The marines—and perhaps the viewing audience watching live on television—didn't have the patience to wait for what would have likely taken the Iraqis all day to do.

A cheer rang out from the crowd when a marine tank rescue vehicle (an armored personnel carrier equipped with a crane used to drag away damaged vehicles and rescue their crews) rolled up to the statue. Several Iraqis jumped on board the armored vehicle—helped up by the marines—as the crew's rigger, standing on the tip of the crane, looped a metal chain around Saddam's throat. The mood among the Iraqis was electric and carnival-like as the statue was pulled down. People were shaking hands with the marines and throwing their shoes at Saddam's face, an especially grave insult in the Arab world. The atmosphere was so hectic and festive that few people, if any, seemed to notice that the marines first put an American flag over Saddam's face, clearly sending the wrong message, before replacing it with an Iraqi one.

After the statue was toppled, I ran down from my perch to grab several marines to put them on air. My first question was a selfish one: "Are you staying?" They were. *Il Hamdu Allah.* To my surprise, the marines said they'd been under the impression that the journalists at the Palestine were being held hostage. The marines had been prepared to fight to take over the building. A sniper told me he almost "double pumped" (two shots through the head) a reporter on one of the hotel's upper floors, suspicious of his laptop.

Watching the statue of Saddam being ripped off its base was for me both exciting—it was delightful to see Iraqis finally venting their anger against the symbol of the man who'd psychologically tortured them for decades—and troubling. The crowd beneath the statue was composed of Shiite

Muslims, who were simultaneously cheering Saddam's demise and demanding a greater role in the future government—on the very first day.

"Yes, yes to freedom and the fall of dictatorship!" they cheered—the words *freedom* and *dictatorship* rhyming in Arabic.

But they also yelled, "Remember Sadr!," a reference to Mohammed Sadiq al-Sadr, one of the most influential Shiite Muslim clerics in Iraq, killed by Saddam's agents in 1999. The late cleric's son, Muqtada al-Sadr, would quickly emerge as one of the most controversial figures in post-war Iraq as he capitalized on growing anti-American frustration to gain popularity among Iraq's Shiites, comprising about 60 percent of the population.

There can be no doubt that most Iraqis in Baghdad were genuinely delighted that the Americans ousted Saddam Hussein. Nearly all of the marines I interviewed were wearing flowers given to them by grateful Iraqis. Baghdadis were so happy the Americans had taken over, in fact, that when several shots were fired at the marines after the Saddam statue was torn down, a small group of people broke off from the pack to hunt down those responsible and kill them.

It's profoundly disappointing, although not altogether surprising, how quickly the Iraqis' joy and appreciation turned to frustration and in some cases hatred of the Americans. I heard the first anti-American rumblings in Baghdad only one day

after the statue came down. The main problem was the shameful looting that broke out as Baghdad collapsed, and the Americans' utter inability to stop it. Many Iraqis have subsequently
accused the US forces of being unwilling to stop the looters
and even of encouraging them, although this isn't true. I was
talking with a tank crew as looters were ransacking the Iraqi
Ministry of Planning. The soldiers and I watched Iraqis haul
away light fixtures, furniture, telephones and anything else they
could tear off the walls. The soldiers were disgusted by what
they were witnessing, but were totally unequipped, unprepared
and untrained to do anything to stop it. The tank crew couldn't
have gotten out of their vehicle and started arresting people
(they didn't have handcuffs or a place to put the detainees, for
starters), nor could they (or should they) have opened fire on
the mobs of thieves. It would have been preferable—I think
essential—if the army and marines had jointly implemented a
round-the-clock curfew for the first several weeks after Baghdad collapsed. The vast majority of Iraqis would have respected
the curfew and even welcomed the move. Most people still had
food in their houses and didn't need to go outside, except to
take the sick and elderly to hospitals, which could have been
arranged. A twenty-four-hour curfew would have stopped
much of the looting, which terrorized the Iraqi people, disillusioned them about the Americans' intentions and caused enormous damage to the Iraqi infrastructure, which then caused
delays in restoring basic services in Baghdad. The army official
who told me that the military had been judicious in bombing

the Iraqi power grid knowing it would have to be rebuilt said much of the trouble the Americans had turning the lights back on in Baghdad was caused by looters, who stole copper wires, switches and everything else they could find. The looting also added billions of dollars and many months to the price tag of rebuilding Iraq, not to mention the irreplaceable antiquities, especially thirty large statues (some of them priceless) carted away from the Baghdad museum.

Implementing a twenty-four-hour curfew in Baghdad was, however, impossible for three reasons: There simply weren't enough US troops to enforce one, the forces didn't have the right training or equipment for the job, and the army and marines didn't communicate well. The first two weaknesses (and perhaps the third as well) continued to plague the US military in Iraq for months.

The army—which never did cross over to the eastern half of Baghdad—established its own small fiefdom on the western shore of the Tigris under its sole jurisdiction. Similarly, the marines emerged as all-powerful in the east. Moving from one side of the river to the other wasn't easy, a fact I discovered when Rageh Omar of the BBC and I tried in vain to organize with the marines an escort for a convoy of about two dozen reporters out of Baghdad after the war. The marines said they'd take us as far as the river, but didn't know how to get in contact with the army on the other side. I ultimately was told to contact US Central Command in Qatar to send a message to the army less than two miles away. Central Command, however, refused to help organize the convoy for reporters who'd been in Baghdad throughout the war, arguing that we were "unilaterals" and that the military was only responsible for journalists who had been "embedded" with the armed forces.

While better communication between the army and marines in Baghdad would have improved the situation, a high-ranking army officer in Iraq told me after the war that in his opinion there simply weren't enough US troops to have ever controlled Baghdad effectively, nor did they have the right tools to do it. The overriding US strategy throughout the war was to take Iraq with a force that was fast, light, lethal and precise. Luckily, it worked with astounding success, but while the "fast and light" strategy destroyed the military and government, it couldn't contain the predictably chaotic aftermath of the war. That was obvious to me as I sat with the tank crew watching the Ministry of Planning being looted. We were sitting on top of a massive state-of-the-art killing machine, but were powerless. A few dozen city cops armed with nothing more than tear gas, riot shields and wooden batons would have been more effective. Having the wrong equipment for what eventually became a police mission would become a major problem in the months after the end of major combat, during which the Americans discovered that the same Abrams tanks that were so useful for smashing Iraqi armor in the desert were essentially useless for patrolling Baghdad, and that their Humvees—fast and efficient when protected by heavy armor and attack helicopters—were sitting ducks when alone in Iraqi towns and cities.

* * *

It's often asked why Baghdad fell with so little resistance. I think it was a combination of the ferocity and effectiveness of the American pre-assault bombardment, a generally poor Iraqi plan to defend the capital and a total lack of will by the Republican Guards to fight for the dying Saddam regime. While it's unfair (and inaccurate) to say that the US military mercilessly pounded Baghdad for twenty nights and days before the troops rolled into town (there were amazingly few civilian deaths caused by the air campaign), the bombardment was without a doubt relentless and crippling. By the time US troops were fighting on the ground for Baghdad, the city was completely without power and telephones, and practically every building belonging to the security services, fedayeen, Baath party and Republican Guard had been flattened. The city was also mostly empty. On the morning of April 8, the once omnipresent Baath party militiamen failed to occupy their posts on street corners. Baghdad was in many ways a defeated city even before the Americans rolled in.

The Iraqi war plan also relied heavily on the Republican Guards to protect Baghdad, according to a ranking member of the elite Iraqi unit, but they proved to be much less committed than Saddam and his government had anticipated. The Iraqi strategy for Baghdad was to allow the Americans to enter the city (the Iraqi leadership didn't believe that the untrained, mostly unpaid Baath militiamen would stand their ground) and then to surround the city with Republican Guards, cutting

off US supply lines and drawing the Americans into street battles, ambushing small units and killing them until the American public demanded an end to the war. The Iraqi leaders were
convinced the US public was not willing to sustain casualties
and that the war was essentially unpopular in the United
States. Senior Iraqi leaders, including someone as rational and
educated as Tareq Aziz, believed the war had been imposed on
the Americans by the Bush family, American oil companies and
Zionists in general.

Saddam Hussein is said to have been profoundly shocked
and saddened when the Republican Guard failed to mobilize a
counterattack. It certainly caught al-Sahaf off guard. Uday al-
Ta'e told me that after he and al-Sahaf fled the Palestine on
April 8, checking into a nearby hotel, the information minister
started pacing the room, waiting for the Republican Guard to
emerge and start fighting.

"Where are they?" he kept asking. "Where are they!"

US military officials say some members of the Republican
Guard had evidently obeyed the leaflets the US air-dropped
during the war in specially adapted "Rockeye bombs" normally designed to release cluster bombs. The leaflets told Iraqis
how to position their weapons to tell the Americans they didn't
want to fight. Other Republican Guards gave up once they saw
that the Americans had already taken control of Baghdad and
that people were celebrating their arrival.

The swift fall of Baghdad shocked the Arab world. As I
left Iraq on April 15, traveling back to the United States
through Jordan, people I met seemed both disappointed and

embarrassed that Baghdad—a fellow Arab and Islamic capi-tal—had fallen to the Americans without a fight. When I trav-eled back to Baghdad ten weeks later, I found the same Jorda-nians celebrating the daily attacks against American soldiers in post-war Iraq. It was their way of saying, "See, I told you it would be difficult."

CHAPTER EIGHT

I GRINNED TO MYSELF on July 2 when I saw US troops manning the checkpoint along the border between Jordan and Iraq where only five months earlier I'd spent so many nervous hours hiding reporting equipment, passing out bribes like lollipops and giving free rides to Iraqi intelligence officers so they'd look the other way at my illegal satellite phone and flak jacket. The GIs, including one very young-looking man who said he was from Florida and had chewing tobacco stuffed into his bulging lower lip, were dressed in camouflage vests and helmets. They were smiling and very affable. "Hey, he's American!" the soldier with dip in his lip yelled to his comrades at the gate, waving me through without inspecting my GMC Suburban. The troops couldn't have been more different from the sinister Iraqi crooks who had worked there before, many of whom—much to my surprise—still had jobs at the checkpoint. My driver leered at one of the former customs/intelligence officials who was acting as a translator/facilitator, according to the handwritten laminated badge pinned to his shirt.

"I know that guy," my driver grumbled under his breath. "If the American soldiers weren't here, I'd kill him." My driver said that for years the customs official had extorted money from him, confiscating (read: stealing) music tapes from his car and demanding that he bring him pornographic CD-ROMs from Baghdad. My driver's rage was a harbinger of what I would soon find in Baghdad, where three decades of bitter scores were being settled one by one. It was also disturbing to see that the Americans were so dependent on Iraqis with shady pasts, although that was almost inevitable, because nearly anyone who had even a little authority under Saddam had created enemies. The alternative would have been for the Americans to have found new employees with no experience for nearly every job, which would have been a logistical nightmare.

I'd never seen the border as crowded as it was on that hot, dusty day. There were hundreds of cars, trucks and trailers jockeying for position in the morning sun. The temperature was already pushing a hundred degrees at ten o'clock. Many of the vehicles trying to cram through the funnel of traffic at the border were window-sticker new, heading into Iraq for sale. It was encouraging because I took the traffic as a sign that the Iraqi economy—strangled by decades of international sanctions, neglect, corruption and mismanagement—was starting to flourish. I saw that small rusty oil tankers, which had formerly driven into Jordan every day full of cheap Iraqi fuel, were still actively engaged in the cross-border trade. From the border, it seemed like business in Iraq was booming.

At the checkpoint, I also met an Iraqi American from the Midwest who was traveling to Baghdad for the first time, in search of his family. He didn't know how many people were alive or what had happened to them. All he had were a few names and an address in a town near Karbala where he thought his extended family lived. He also made me optimistic about Iraq's future, and I was genuinely excited to see what had happened in Iraq. I was upbeat despite what I'd heard about the growing frustration Iraqis were feeling toward the Americans and the increasing number of attacks against US forces. I figured it was just part of Iraq's growing pains. I still do.

Little had visibly changed along the desert road between Jordan and Baghdad since I'd left just after the main battles ended. The burned-out carcasses of Iraqi armored vehicles, along with scores of charred and bullet-ridden civilian cars and buses, were still scattered along the highway like roadkill.

When I pulled into Baghdad, however, it was obvious that much had changed in the ten weeks I'd been away. I saw TV satellite dishes, long forbidden by the Iraqi government, for sale on practically every major commercial street. Iraqis could now watch al-Jazeera and Al-Arabiya (a new Arabic news channel that's even more controversial and politically charged than al-Jazeera) for the first time, in addition to pornographic movies from Eastern Europe.

In Baghdad, stores sold Thuraya telephones, handheld satellite phones with GSM and GPS functions, which had once been the emblem of all that was verboten by the former government. Six people accused of spying were executed at the Abu Greib prison two days before the first bombs fell on Baghdad primarily because they'd been caught with Thuraya phones, according to a former prison guard. Iraq had been especially sensitive about the Thuraya because its calls are difficult to trace and because the phone's GPS locator makes it a useful targeting device.

Driving into a chaotic Baghdad intersection, I also saw an old man hawking about a dozen newspapers pinned under his arm. He was desperately trying to make change before his customer sped away. I eagerly bought all the papers he had. They were all new and had optimistic, forward-looking titles like *The Dawn of Baghdad*, *The Renaissance* and *The New Iraq*. Over the next few days, I discovered that nearly every Iraqi with the slightest bit of political ambition seemed to have opened a newspaper after Saddam's fall, including Mohammed al-Hamdani, whom I first met at one of the three pastry shops he owned, famous for its little barrel-shaped filo-dough sweets filled with cheese and smothered in honey. They're called women's upper arms because of their chunky, tube-like shape, much like al-Hamdani himself.

Al-Hamdani's day job was still managing his pastry shops, but after hours he went to the office where he'd set up new computers and a dozen reporters. Al-Hamdani called his newspaper *Those Who Have Been Freed*. Like most of the new Iraqi newspapers, *Those Who Have Been Freed* was tabloid size, opinionated and highly critical of everyone and everything. Most of the articles and editorials in the eight-page newspaper reflected a blend of fiery Iraqi nationalism, grassroots socialism and Islamic fundamentalism. This cocktail of political thinking seemed to be emerging as the most popular political outlook in post-war Iraq. If there had been a newspaper or political party called something like The Islamic Union of Conspiratorial Disgruntled Patriotic Iraqis, I think it would have been right on the money.

Like most newspapers, *Those Who Have Been Freed* denounced the American occupation authority and, even more vociferously, its competitors, the other new newspapers in Baghdad. The spite the new newspapers expressed for one another was venomous and they routinely accused one another of stealing stories, having links to the Baath party or simply of theft.

Only a few months earlier, it would have been impossible for al-Hamdani—a proud man in his forties with an easy smile and a squat build—to have opened a newspaper. There had only been a handful of state-run newspapers under Saddam and all of their chief editors had been closely scrutinized by the Iraqi intelligence agencies. Now, there were several hundred completely unregulated newspapers. Al-Hamdani said it was impossible to know exactly how many newspapers there were because twenty were born each week while another ten closed. He told me that Iraq was going through what he called its *infitah* or "opening"—Iraq's version of Glasnost, which opened the Soviet Union two decades earlier.

I went with al-Hamdani to the press where each week he printed three thousand copies of his newspaper on a gorgeous, loud, foul-smelling, diesel-powered German machine—perfectly maintained since the 1970s—that printed single sheets at a time. Al-Hamdani had a pistol tucked in his belt, worried that hit men hired by the rival newspapers he slammed would try to kill him. Iraq certainly now had freedom of expression, but it was tainted with chaos. It's been said that freedom of expression does not include the freedom to yell "Fire!" in a crowded theater; Iraq now had *that* kind of freedom of expression.

Some of the newspapers were blatantly irresponsible, and there was even one that specialized in selling stolen property. I understood why the US administration in Iraq—at this stage led by Ambassador L. Paul Bremer III—closed down several newspapers after they'd printed what amounted to death threats against US and Iraqi officials. Iraqis had never had a free press before and had a lot of pent-up anger they wanted to release. The result was an explosion of printed words. The new freedom also meant Iraqis could learn about the abuses and excesses of their former government for the first time.

There was a mob huddled around a television set outside a store selling DVDs on al-Rashid Street, named for the legendary Caliph Haroun al-Rashid described in the famous *Thousand and One Nights* set in Baghdad twelve hundred years ago. The television set was playing one of the new CDs the shop had for sale. The CD showed about twenty Iraqi men in army uniforms standing at attention in a line. They were barefoot. A big man was in front of them wearing a green uniform and a beret. He called out the name of the first man on the line, a skinny soldier who looked about twenty-five, who came to the center of a courtyard of what seemed to be a military base. He lay flat on his back and raised his feet. Two guards grabbed hold of his ankles and wrapped leather straps fixed to a log around them, turning the log to tighten the bindings. The guards held the log between them like a limbo stick, exposing the soles of the man's feet to the big man in the beret, who started whipping them viciously with a cane. The man being punished for crimes unknown writhed in pain, screaming, flailing on his back, flapping his arms against the pavement, rolling back and forth as his feet were beaten relentlessly. The other soldiers waiting in line watched in silence, knowing they were next. After the man was lashed about fifty times, he was released from the fetters, stood up quickly but uneasily and hobbled to the back of the line, teetering as he went, obviously trying to put weight on only the sides of his feet.

It turned out, however, that his punishment wasn't finished. After two more men were caned, the man in the beret summoned back the first man for another round of beatings. The young soldier let out an agonizing yelp—high-pitched like a wounded animal's—when the cane slapped against the soles of his feet for the first time during the second round. The people in the crowd on the street watching him scream were visibly empathizing with him; some people were covering their mouths and nearly everyone was shaking his head in disappointment, but not in disbelief. All Iraqis knew that during thirty years of dictatorship many human rights abuses had been committed. In fact, several people in the crowd had been tortured by the former regime themselves. That was the very reason, they said, that they wanted to buy copies of the video of the men being caned. They wanted to share their experience, an important part of overcoming psychological trauma and post-traumatic stress syndrome. By buying the CD of the men being abused, the Iraqis were in many ways self-medicating. Other Iraqis were just incredibly curious. The CD was a big moneymaker for the store's owner, Samir Fuleyeh, who sold as many as four hundred copies of it a day for fifty cents apiece. Fuleyeh said he bought the original tape from looters who'd stolen it from an Iraqi intelligence headquarters. The beatings had been videotaped so that whoever had ordered the punishment would know that his instructions had been carried out. It was, it turns out, a common practice in Iraq.

I saw another videotape of one of Saddam's surgeons amputating a man's hand, his punishment for dealing in dollars contrary to a government order. The videotape was in the possession of an Iraqi man who owned a VHS-repair shop. He said intelligence agents had come to his shop to make a copy of the tape and that he'd secretly made a dub for himself after he was horrified by what he saw. The amputation punishment—removing the right hand of the gold dealer who'd traded in dollars—was taped in its entirety. It started with the surgeon drawing over the veins and arteries in the wrist with colored magic markers, showed the scalpel cutting away healthy tissue and finished with a guard holding up the severed hand by a single finger for the camera.

There were also videos of executions for sale. In one, several men were taken out to a desert. Iraqis in military uniforms sat the first man against a dune and slipped a black canvas bag over his head. One of the men in uniform then walked up to the condemned man and stuffed a fist-sized bundle of plastic explosives into the breast pocket of his shirt. The camera showed the man sitting alone on the sand for about thirty agonizing seconds, his hands tied behind his back, until the explosives were detonated, blowing his body in half and tossing up a cloud of smoke and sand. The men in uniform then sat the next person to be killed beside the remains of the previous victim (only the lower half of the torso and legs were visible), slipped explosives in his shirt pocket and repeated the process. Watching this tape—obviously too hideous to broadcast on American television—made me queasy and my hands shake; I was appalled at what brutal, stupid cowards human beings can be. But even more disturbing than seeing men blown to hamburger (there was no possible reason to carry out an execution in this way; somebody must have just liked the idea of putting plastic explosives in a man's shirt) was watching the Iraqi officers carrying out the murders and listening to their ambivalent chitchat. The men were casually smoking cigarettes and complaining about problems they'd evidently been having with their cars. They were trying to figure out rides back home and were completely oblivious and indifferent to the men they were destroying. The nineteenth-century historian Lord John Acton famously wrote, "Power tends to corrupt, and absolute power corrupts absolutely." I'd add that when you strip away all fear of repercussions and give people the option of saying they were just carrying out orders, the result is corruption coupled with barbarism and sadism; that was Iraq under Saddam.

Iraq's new freedom also meant that people could openly talk about Saddam himself, including those close to the former dictator, like Ibrahim al-Basri, Saddam's physician. In the early 1970s, al-Basri had been one of the best-known doctors in Iraq. Pictures of him from the time show a cocky, handsome, self-described ladies' man wearing open-necked shirts that exposed a forest of inky chest hair. Al-Basri had his own fitness program on Iraqi television. Tapes of the broadcast showed him flanked by women in brightly colored zip-up training suits doing calisthenics to music. Al-Basri told me he may not have been the best doctor in Iraq in the 1970s, but he was probably the most famous.

"That's why Saddam picked me," he said. "Saddam liked to be surrounded by famous people. It made him feel like he was getting the best."

Saddam also respected al-Basri's confidence, the doctor said, appreciating that he didn't cower in the Iraqi leader's presence like so many of his bootlicking underlings. When Saddam offered al-Basri a seat in his office, al-Basri said he took it, unlike some government ministers who would tell Saddam, "No, sir. I could never think of sitting in your presence."

Al-Basri said Saddam suffered from chronic back pain and that his main responsibility was giving him steroid injections and supervising the swimming that was central to his physical therapy. Saddam was an excellent patient who followed his medical regimen strictly and took his health very seriously. Saddam also had an extremely volatile personality and could be affable and avuncular one moment, cruel, brutal and vindictive the next.

I sat with al-Basri in an oddly decorated room in his large house in Baghdad. It was al-Basri's barroom and it hadn't been rearranged since his heyday in the 1970s. The room was stuck in time, and was complete with a sunken seating area, a bamboo-faced bar with swivel-topped stools, brown carpeting on the floor and walls, and an old guitar propped in the corner. The reason the décor hadn't changed was that al-Basri had spent the last thirteen years in prison. Saddam had al-Basri jailed because he refused to become a member of Iraq's parliament. Al-Basri described how an old friend had visited him in 1990, saying he had "good news" for the doctor.

"The leader president has asked you to run for parliament," al-Basri was told.

"What for?" al-Basri replied. "I don't want to just raise my hand all day long," he said, referring to the main duty of the rubber-stamp parliament, which was to unanimously approve everything Saddam asked for.

Al-Basri's friend reported him to the secret police, along

with al-Basri's East German wife and son because they'd been in the room at the time, heard the conversation but didn't turn him in, and were therefore party to the insult. Al-Basri was sentenced to life in prison. His son and wife were given ten and two years respectively.

Al-Basri was shuttled between the massive Abu Greib prison complex and a small, horrible jail in the center of Baghdad operated by the intelligence service that held political prisoners. It was one of the darkest corners of humanity.

Tears welled up in al-Basri's eyes when we walked into what had been his tiny cell at the al-Hakimeya jail for political prisoners. The cell was a tiny, airless room where he'd slept on the floor with more than ten other inmates. There was a toilet—just a hole in floor—at the back of the room, which al-Basri said had stunk and been infested with cockroaches that would climb into his nose at night. Al-Basri was only issued one pajama suit by the prison and was constantly covered in lice, which he said he would pick off his body and crush against the wall to write messages of hope and leave a record of his existence, knowing that any day he could be killed or die from disease.

I saw the sad testimonies "We all die" and "God help me" written on the walls.

When the toilet in the cell was full, Al-Basri said his cellmates would urinate in the one plastic bowl they were given to eat from collectively, and then throw the piss into the hall through a mailbox-slot-size ventilation slit in the cell's metal door. Al-Basri said the conditions in the cell were so unsanitary, stuffy and cramped that the flesh in his underarms and groin rotted away. He said the worst experience, however, was when prisoners were taken out of the cell for interrogation and beaten for hours before being thrown back into the cell.

"What are we to do with him?" al-Basri had asked a guard after he'd tossed an unconscious prisoner back into the cell following an interrogation.

"Fuck him," the guard yelled back.

Al-Basri described how the guards would sexually humiliate the prisoners, forcing them to strip naked, tying two of them together face-to-face and making them dance.

As we were leaving the prison, I was surprised that al-Basri ran into two former inmates lingering in the hallway. Ironically, they were now working at the jail, which had become a makeshift headquarters of the Supreme Council for Islamic Revolution in Iraq, an Iranian-backed Shiite Muslim party led by Ayatollah Mohammed Bakr al-Hakim, who was soon to be assassinated. The Shiite group—forbidden under Saddam and responsible for bomb attacks in Baghdad—had simply taken over the empty building. I remember thinking that it must not have been particularly healthy for the sanity of the former prisoners to be working in the dungeon where they'd been so abused.

After the war, al-Basri founded a human rights group for victims of Saddam's regime. The man who had once cared for Saddam was now caring for those whose lives Saddam had destroyed.

* * *

Others close to Saddam, including his cook, maid and fortune-teller, were also now free to talk. A maid who'd worked at Baghdad's main Republican Palace (which after the war became the seat of the US administration in Iraq) described her boss as a hypochondriac, obsessed with cleanliness. Like all of the palace's staff, she underwent a complete physical examination—including tests of her blood, urine and stool—every two months. She said anyone with the slightest malady was immediately fired, and that Saddam preferred to hire Iraqi Christians and older women, saying they were cleaner and more reliable. She described how she was required to step on a mat impregnated with a disinfectant before entering Saddam's bedroom, and to polish his fruit and dinner plates with single-use sterilized cloths before serving his food on them.

One of Saddam's cooks said the former Iraqi dictator didn't like too much salt on his food and that he was concerned about his weight, forbidding the cook from using butter or ghee, preferring vegetable oil. The cook, a short jolly man with thick strong hands, said Saddam had simple tastes and enjoyed eating grilled meats and fish, stewed vegetables and rice, and dates for dessert. The cook said Saddam developed an incentive system to ensure quality meals, fining him roughly five to ten dollars if he was unsatisfied with the food, and rewarding him anywhere from five to a hundred dollars if the meal was to his liking. The cook said he was only scared once during six years of service at the Republican Palace, when Saddam became ill after one of his meals. Luckily, he was cleared of charges of trying to poison Saddam.

People close to Saddam also said the former Iraqi dictator was deeply interested in the occult and regularly consulted fortune-tellers and clairvoyants, including a thirteen-year-old boy who Saddam believed could see through walls and read minds. His job was to make sure no one close to Saddam was plotting against him. Saddam was also said to have worn a stone around his left arm to make him bulletproof, according to the members of Iraq's Mandean community—a small religious group who believe that Adam was the first prophet—who sold him the rock.

Iraq's *infitah* was also a political awakening, and during the weeks I'd been out of the country, two hundred new political parties had sprung up. Before Saddam's fall, there had only been the Baath party, and Iraqis had obviously been thirsting for more. With no registration process, all any Iraqi needed to do to start a party was put up a sign and, evidently, open a newspaper. I saw hand-painted signs plastered on buildings across Baghdad, spray-painted hastily on walls (the names painted so haphazardly they sometimes looked like little more than graffiti) and written on bedsheets hanging outside the windows of apartment blocks, marking the headquarters of new parties, political unions, professional syndicates and human rights groups. Many of the parties seemed to be loyal to one of the main Shiite Muslim *merja*—senior Shiite clerics—who exercise more control over their followers than most Sunni Muslim imams. The fear that the Shiite's merja, who have been tolerant of the US occupation, could turn has hung over the American administration since its arrival in Baghdad. Looking at the parties emerging in Iraq, it was clear that the strategic Shiite population was starting to spread its wings after decades of repression.

Other new political parties were communist, nationalist, royalist (supporting the return of the Hashemite monarchy to Iraq) and independent. The new political dynamism was palpable, and ideas were hotly debated at Baghdad cafés and on college campuses by people like history professor Ali al-Nashmi.

Al-Nashmi hadn't yet hung up his sign when I first met him at the empty building he was converting into his personal kingdom. A highly ambitious man, he gave me a tour of the new office space—stepping over a workman scraping droplets of paint off the stone floor—explaining the layout of the future headquarters of his new political party (the Union of Independent Intellectuals), socialist newspaper (*The Dawn of Baghdad*), magazine for children (as yet unnamed) and, he hoped, local television station.

Like al-Hamdani—who'd always dreamed of a life beyond his honey-covered "women's upper arms"—al-Nashmi was bursting with pent-up political desires. Twenty years earlier, al-Nashmi had been arrested and tortured by Saddam's regime for starting a movie club in his home, where about a dozen of his friends would gather in secret every week to watch and discuss foreign films. Al-Nashmi was first accused of founding an illegal communist cell and later of being an Islamic militant, a charge that seemed especially ill-suited, considering his secular views, Western dress and polished English. Al-Nashmi languished behind bars for three years, a relatively short sentence by Iraqi standards. Once, he said, he was beaten so severely during an interrogation—hit with fists and batons—that his entire body was black and blue, preventing him from sleeping, or even moving, without pain for days. Al-Nashmi was determined that such abuses shouldn't be repeated and had gathered about 150 similarly minded intellectuals and professors to start his party.

The fact that al-Nashmi was building a headquarters was something of an anomaly in post-war Iraq. Other parties had simply taken over former government buildings the way al-Hakim's Supreme Council for Islamic Revolution in Iraq had set up shop in the intelligence services' jail and at Tareq Aziz's palatial home along the Tigris, which Aziz no longer needed because he was in US custody at the airport, terrified that the Americans would turn him over to an Iraqi court. Ahmed Chalabi—the leader of the previously exiled Iraqi National Congress—moved into the house of Saddam's advisor Ezzat Ibrahim, a swank villa designed to look like a Japanese palace complete with a footbridge. Ibrahim didn't need it; the man who'd compared Saddam to the Prophet Mohammed was on the run. The Iraqi people considered him Saddam's most loyal cadre, a man who'd been so eager to please his boss as to be laughable. He'd long been the butt of Iraqi jokes, which people were now able to tell openly for the first time.

One day Saddam Hussein decides to go to a poor market disguised as a woman to find out what ordinary people really think about him. He goes up to an old woman selling cream and says, "Kind old woman, how much for your cream?"

The old woman answers, "For you, my lord, it's free!"

"What?" Saddam says, completely surprised. "Why do you call me 'my lord'? Please just tell me how much for your cream?"

But the old woman insists, "I could never take money from you, my lord!"

Saddam gets annoyed and asks, "How do you know who I am?"

Then the old woman pulls off her wig and says, "It's me—Ezzat! Don't you recognize me?"

There were new jokes about Saddam too.

God sends an angel to earth to collect Saddam's soul. Normally, angels are quick, and come back right away. But after a month there's still no word from him.

So God sends another angel to find out what happened to the first one. Later that day, the second angel returns with a sad look on his face. God asks him, "Did you find the first angel I sent?"

"Yes, Lord, I did," he replies. "He'd been asking questions about Saddam, and now they've got him locked up at the General Security Service headquarters."

Shortly after my return to Baghdad, I attended a conference at the former lawyers syndicate organized by forty of the new political parties. As soon as I walked in the door, I was besieged by new party leaders and their often pert female personal assistants who obliged me to promise to visit their headquarters, have tea and learn more about (read: promote) their activities. The hot topic at the conference was the formation of the twenty-five-member Iraqi governing council. Most of the parties at the conference complained that Bremer's administration had given too much authority to "foreign" parties like Chalabi's Iraqi National Congress.

Although I was surprised at the prominent role given to Chalabi, considering the widespread accusations of corruption and graft against him in the Arab world, I was generally impressed with the United States' selection of the council members. The council was not the toothless group of US lackeys and sycophants I'd suspected the American administration would have preferred to have appointed. Instead, the Bremer administration hadn't shied away from appointing Iraqi Muslim leaders and other people who harbored deep suspicions about the United States and its policies in the Middle East. I have some doubts, however, about whether the US administration fully realizes what it created, giving huge authority to the Shiite merja and the Shiite Daawa (Islamic call) party, a previously militant movement Saddam had brutally and systematically crushed. I thought the United States' appointments to the council were very courageous.

But no matter what the United States did, the Iraqis weren't happy. After a few months in Iraq, I was becoming frustrated by the constant complaining I heard. Iraqis—who'd been told

what to do and what to think for decades—suddenly had opinions about everything. It became impossible to turn on a television camera on a busy street in Baghdad without a crowd of
people forming, yelling: "Where's our electricity? Where's our
security? Where is the aid the Americans promised us?"

Sometimes I told people, "Yes, you're right. The Americans aren't doing anything right. They should re-appoint Saddam." I'd watch the life drain out of their faces.

While more could be done to improve the infrastructure in
Iraq, I believe there is a fundamental reason why the Iraqis are
so dissatisfied and feel so insecure. It's because they can finally
vent their frustrations, speak freely and know that someone is
listening. They are scared not just because of the increase of
crime and bombings, but also because they don't know what
will happen to Iraq and who will run it.

The Americans also opened themselves up to the avalanche
of criticism by taking on the task of radically restructuring
Iraqi society and fighting an often brutal guerilla war while
giving the Iraqis the freedom to openly comment on what's
going on around them. It's the correct, but also the most difficult approach.

Iraqis had unrealistic expectations of what the Americans
would and could do after the war. After watching the US military crush what they'd been told was the powerful Iraqi
armed forces, most Iraqis simply couldn't accept that the
same US military wasn't able to turn on the lights in Baghdad
or arrest a few thieves. It was the same disbelief I'd seen at
the al-Shaab market when it was bombed during the war

when people assumed American missiles couldn't have been misdirected or malfunctioned and therefore suspected the United States of foul play. Many Iraqis now concluded that the United States *wanted* Iraq to remain in chaos in order to keep it weak, thereby easing the US/Zionist plot to plunder the nation's oil, a belief fueled by the shameful fact that the Oil Ministry was one of a few buildings the US military secured after entering Baghdad.

Although I was energized to see so much freedom in Iraq, I realized that Iraqis can't live on freedom alone. They need jobs and security too, because without them there's no way to enjoy liberty. This point was driven home when I looked up Ali.

I found Ali even more shy than usual. He smiled demurely when he saw me in the coffee shop of the hotel where I was staying, but I could tell he was depressed. I excitedly asked him how he was, and if he was still working with reporters. He said he couldn't work anymore because he'd been car-jacked at gunpoint. The white Toyota Super that he'd driven throughout the war hadn't survived the initial months of peace. Ali told me he had grown tired of working in danger-ous situations and was considering taking a job at a neigh-bor's clothing shop for almost no money. He seemed utterly apathetic. The post-war chaos and crime wave had trauma-tized Ali more than the war itself.

Since the fall of Baghdad on April 9, car theft, murder and rape have skyrocketed. The lawlessness was evident at the Al-Dora police station. At 8 A.M. on the day I spent as an observer at the station, Lieutenant Colonel Ala'a Hassan—a stocky twenty-year veteran cop in his late forties—started his shift by taking a report about a stolen 1997 Datsun. There were 380,000 people in his precinct and he had only a hundred officers, one telephone, two patrol cars and a pickup truck to provide them protection. There had been 60,000 police in Baghdad before the war. By mid-September, there was only a quarter of that number, although the US administration in Iraq has actively been recruiting more.

At 10:55 A.M., a grandmother walked into Lt. Col. Hassan's Spartan white office crying. She told Hassan that she'd accepted a ride from a man after she'd gotten off a bus, finding it too crowded. When she offered the man some money, however, he stole $500 from her purse, the equivalent of almost half a year's wages for most Iraqis.

"It's your fault," Hassan yelled. "You shouldn't get into a car with strangers! The situation here now isn't stable." He was frustrated. He felt powerless, and he was venting on the victim.

An hour later, a policeman told Hassan that a patrol searching for unexploded ordnance had discovered a decomposed body hidden among reeds growing along a nearby road. The body stunk like sewage when we arrived in the station's pickup truck to collect it. It was broken in three pieces and had been partially eaten by animals and insects. The police, paid $120 a month, unenthusiastically put the body in a cardboard box and carted it away. They were disgusted by the stench, but not surprised to have found a corpse tossed along the side of the road. They assumed the crime was a revenge killing, which had become commonplace.

Iraqi newspapers were full of articles of old grudges being settled. One told the story of a farmer who'd become enraged in the late 1990s in the southern city of Basra when a bureaucrat at the government Health Ministry ignored his plea for medicine for his sick cow. The farmer believed he was given the runaround because he wasn't a Baath party member or anyone important. After the war, the farmer tracked down the former bureaucrat and demanded that he pay for the cow; otherwise, the farmer threatened, he'd kill him. In Baghdad, there was a story of a bulldozer operator who'd demolished three homes of Shiite Muslims in the early 1990s on orders from the government. After the war he was approached by their relatives, who said that unless he paid for new houses, he'd pay with his life. There was no need to bluff in Baghdad, because it was easy to get away with murder. In fact, murders had become so pervasive—there were as many as seven hundred a month in Baghdad, fourteen times as many as in New York City—that one happened in front of my hotel.

A man walked up to a car, talked to a man inside it for a few minutes and then shot him in the head before escaping in a waiting vehicle. People in the neighborhood came onto the street after the shots were fired, brandishing their own guns in front of their homes and stores and squeezing off a few rounds in the air to show that they were serious. After about twenty minutes, an Iraqi police patrol arrived on the scene, but kept on driving after seeing all the armed people in the streets. The body of the murdered man remained slumped over in the car for about twelve hours, until US troops came by and took it away. I have no idea what motivated the murderer, but I was struck by how easy it had been. It made me feel as if I were a potential victim, and I wasn't alone. Iraqi women, fearing kidnap and rape, were wearing Islamic veils more than before, hoping the head coverings would make them less tempting to assailants. Iraqi men were applying the same logic to their cars. I saw several pickup trucks in Baghdad had been taken apart—the flatbeds and doors removed—making them less valuable and therefore less likely to be stolen. It was all too much for Ali. Although he'd always been withdrawn, he'd become numb since the end of the war. The enthusiasm I'd seen on his face the day the statue of Saddam was pulled down had vanished. Ali had once thought that as soon as the Saddam system was destroyed, Iraqis wouldn't have to live in fear. Instead, Iraqis had new fears, and Ali had pulled further into his shell.

Zafar, my fat greedy driver from the Flowers Land Hotel, was the next person from the war days I looked up. When we met for coffee Zafar was typically saccharine and obsequious. He showered me with compliments, telling me how much he'd missed me and that his days "had been long without me." After returning similarly insincere flattery, I asked Zafar how he'd held up during the war. I felt somewhat guilty when he told me his brother had been killed by an artillery shell that had fallen on his house. Zafar didn't know if the Americans or the Iraqis had been responsible. Oddly, Zafar didn't seem to be angry about his brother's death. He'd accepted it as God's will and moved on. He had other grievances.

Zafar had dreamed of the windfalls of cash he expected to flow into Iraq after Saddam and international sanctions were removed. He'd imagined that shortly after the war, Iraq would be surfing to prosperity on its ocean of underground oil. But now, even though Saddam was gone, Zafar was both out of a job and deeply in debt. He felt cheated out of Iraq's American dream, which he'd bet money on. A few days after Baghdad fell to the Americans, Zafar sold his hideous Brazili and bought a white Toyota Super, the same model stolen from Ali. Zafar said he'd borrowed the money for the car from a neighbor, whom he implied had looted the cash from a bank. But four months later, Zafar didn't have any customers despite his new car. The reception desk at the Flowers Land Hotel, Zafar said, had stopped referring customers to him. He felt betrayed. He leaned in close to me and stared into my eyes as he lamented his financial woes, clearly hinting I should send some business his way. But I had no intention of using Zafar again. I'd learned that he'd been working for the Iraqi intelligence service during the war. A manager at the Flowers Land had told me that no one at the hotel had ever trusted Zafar and that they'd all been scared of him. He'd been forced on them. I remembered Zafar's threat to expose my conversation with Mohammed the computer hacker about his feelings toward Saddam if I didn't pay him, and understood the Iraqis' desire for revenge.

Of all my acquaintances before the war, Mohammed the computer hacker was the only one clearly benefiting from the collapse of the Saddam system. He'd parlayed his computer skills, perfect English and street smarts into a job at the *Los Angeles Times* as a translator/fixer/computer engineer, earning ten times what he'd made at the Flowers Land. He deserved it. I felt Zafar too deserved what he got, and I was somewhat pleased that his past sins of intimidation (which he'd wrongly assumed would be forgiven and forgotten) were catching up with him.

Zafar told me his economic situation was increasingly desperate because his neighbor was demanding that he repay the loan. He said he could barely afford staples like meat and propane, which nearly every Iraqi family uses to cook.

Iraqis in general weren't prepared for the harsh Darwinian realities of Iraq's new unregulated economy, which was another part of the chaotic freedom the war brought. Landlords, for example, long shackled by laws forbidding them to evict tenants or raise rents, had started tossing people out of their homes, sometimes using armed militiamen to do the dirty work. Iraqis had also been accustomed to job security under Saddam. Under the former regime, practically every Iraqi citizen was employed by either a government bureaucracy or the armed forces. Although salaries had been extremely low—$20 to $60 a month for many civil servants—so were prices, with most staples like soap, cooking oil, flour and beans heavily subsidized by the state. Although the US administration in Iraq continued the subsidy system after the war, the rising prices of non-subsidized items like meat and cooking fuel pushed people into poverty. Iraqis had no choice but to spend their savings, because for the first six months after the war more than half of them were unemployed.

Iraqis were placed in the awkward position of both blaming the Americans for their new woes and simultaneously seeking their help. With nowhere to go, evicted tenants or newly impoverished Iraqis would often turn to American soldiers they saw on the streets for assistance, not really comprehending their role, which was understandable since the soldiers didn't really understand it either. I saw it happen many times. Most of the soldiers would try to be helpful (some more than others) and direct the Iraqis to offices they thought could help them. But often the problems they brought to the soldiers were too complicated or too basic (like "please find me a job") for the troops to deal with. I felt sorry for both the Iraqis and the soldiers, inundated by people with countless grievances and tales of woe, most of them both legitimate and tragic. I saw a single mother complain to a soldier that she didn't have electricity in her house despite having paid a man (a con man) a bribe that he'd promised would get the Americans to switch on the power. The woman—whose husband had abandoned her and her three attractive daughters when he'd traveled to Eastern Europe in search of a job in the early 1980s—was asking why the Americans hadn't made good on their deal. Another Iraqi man wanted a soldier to help him receive compensation for his house, which had been destroyed during the 1991 Gulf War. The soldiers weren't trained to handle this. They were prepared to fight battles and operate military equipment and computers, not to navigate the intricacies of Iraqi culture and sort out decades of accumulated catastrophes. The US soldiers were not police, nor did they have Arabic-language training or the experience to deal with Iraqi/Arab culture and traditions, a shortcoming that would often provoke misunderstandings and, in the worst of cases, drive Iraqis to join the motley mix of criminals, Baath party loyalists, fedayeen, Sunni Muslim fundamentalists, and foreign fighters carrying out attacks against American troops and anyone else they perceived to be a threat.

CHAPTER NINE

THERE IS NO CENTRALLY COMMANDED resistance movement in Iraq, nor a secret rebel army led by Saddam Hussein and his supporters that has been killing US soldiers almost every day. A US military intelligence official told me he wished Iraqi fighters were better coordinated in the post-war period because it would make it easier for the United States to stop them. Instead, US troops and military police—who've played a largely underreported role in battling militant groups—have been struggling to break up dozens of armed, independent yet often interlinked cells that have sprung up in central and western Iraq. There are not hundreds of them either. I estimate, based on interviews with military commanders in several regions of Iraq and with Iraqis involved with these groups, that there are only about fifty to seventy-five of these little bands of fighters, constituting a standing enemy force of about fifteen hundred to five thousand people at any given time. But their easy access to truly massive stockpiles of plastic explosives, mortars and rocket-propelled grenades, and their ability to adapt and forge alliances have made them a tough, scrappy foe, clearly capable of picking off US soldiers, shooting down helicopters and setting off car and truck bombs. The militant cells are often quirky gangs that include both supporters of the former regime and Sunni Muslim extremists, an odd mixture of personalities, to say the least.

The groups work by constantly harassing US forces whenever they are on the move. They most often attack convoys, striking the unprotected Humvees and then running away. According to a military intelligence officer operating in western Iraq, the fighters are often broken into small teams of eight to ten "core" members. These core militants are the brains, moral/spiritual leaders, plotters and holders of purse strings within the gang. They rarely carry out attacks themselves, instead paying underlings to do the dangerous dirty work. They usually choose weak, sometimes stupid, poor farmers or ex-soldiers (almost all of whom are now unemployed) motivated by both the $30 to $50 they receive per attack and a vague sense that they are doing the right thing for God and Iraq.

The Americans have detained thousands of suspects and have been using both psychological and physical pressure to extract intelligence from them. One military official told me he would order captured men to be put in a room and then burst in looking angry, a scowl on his face to show he meant business. He'd start yelling and pointing at the detainees: "You, you and you, Guantanamo Bay!" Soldiers would haul the men who'd been selected out of the room, leaving the others to stew in their imaginations—a marination process he said tends to loosen lips.

"They're all terrified of Guantanamo Bay and think that we're gonna take them there and that they'll never see their families again," the officer said.

Other times, the troops break down a suspect's resistance by not letting him sleep for several days. It's disorienting, debilitating and makes the detainees more malleable. On especially dastardly occasions, detainees are forced to listen to the *Sesame Street* theme song at high volume over and over again until they crack. The music of Metallica, I've been told, has also been effective.

But the detainees often don't have much valuable information. The triggermen are generally very low on the groups' food chain and generally don't know much about the core members. The core members hold the triggermen in such low regard, in fact, that in one case in Falluja, about thirty miles west of Baghdad, the US military discovered that the militant leaders were printing counterfeit Iraqi dinars and paying their gunmen with the bogus notes.

The resistance groups have been operating almost exclusively in an area of Iraq where only about 20 percent of the people live: the Sunni triangle, roughly the size of the state of New Jersey. The fact that the attacks have been carried out by Sunni Muslims in the region where they live—stretching from neighborhoods in Baghdad in the south, the city of Ramadi (near Falluja) to the west and parts of Mosul in the north—proves that the resistance is not the widespread, popular spontaneous uprising by the Iraqi people against the American occupation that the militants claim it is.

It was the fedayeen, Saddam's gang of thugs he'd spoiled and protected, who did most of the fighting against American troops immediately after the fall of Baghdad, although local Sunni Muslim fanatics, and later, foreign Islamic militants quickly made the Iraqi resistance movement their own. In July—when the resistance groups were just starting to make their transformation from secular nationalists to nationalist Islamists—I met a man in his early twenties who was trying to distance himself from a small band of fighters who'd been lobbing grenades and launching rocket-propelled grenades at US soldiers stationed in Baghdad's al-Azamiya neighborhood, a former Saddam stronghold. Al-Azamiya is the heart of Baghdad's Sunni Muslim population, centered around the tomb of Abu Hanifa, an eighth-century Sunni Muslim jurist and scholar. The tomb is commonly referred to as the al-Azamiya mosque. Fighting had been intense in al-Azamiya during the final days of the war, and in a gesture rich with symbolism, Saddam Hussein made his last public appearance in front of the al-Azamiya mosque on April 9 as American tanks were rolling through other parts of Baghdad. The young man I met, himself a former fedayeen, didn't get along with the person who'd recently emerged as his group's new leader, an extremist Sunni Muslim. My contact described him as a follower of the hardline, politically charged *Wahhabi* school of Islamic teaching based in Saudi Arabia. My contact was the polar opposite of a Wahhabi, who, like followers of the *Salafi* school of "purist" Muslim thought, believe that Islam has digressed from the original teachings and practices of the Prophet Mohammed.

My fedayeen from al-Azamiya drank beer, chain-smoked and had little interest in the constant prayer sessions or overbearing religiosity that the gang's new capo was imposing. He said his group consisted of about a dozen "resistance fighters," four of whom were fedayeen. Two others were fugitives, men who'd fled military service under Saddam and had been surviving through petty crime since then. Three others were Sunni religious extremists who thought fighting the Americans was a jihad to protect the sanctity of the al-Azamiya neighborhood. Two others were merely teenagers who enjoyed the lifestyle of being in a gang and were having fun organizing and carrying out clandestine attacks. The final member was the new leader, a dogmatic self-appointed cleric who idealized Osama bin Laden and pretended to be an intellectual, although he had no formal religious training. This little group's motivations for attacks were amazingly parochial and local. They'd just thrown a grenade at an American Bradley because, my contact maintained, a soldier sitting on the turret had been reading a pornographic magazine, which he allegedly enjoyed using to shock Iraqi women as they walked by. True or not, this group—all Sunni Muslims—believed it.

The fedayeen, arguably, had lost the most from Saddam's fall. The young men had been feared under Saddam, and had enjoyed throwing their weight around. The fedayeen had behaved like the ultimate neighborhood bullies, benefiting from the spoils of fear, which can look like respect. Under Saddam, people had always talked politely to the fedayeen, which is extremely important in Arab society, especially to these young men, who were inevitably from poor areas. The fedayeen also had the power to steal and sometimes to rape women without repercussions. Those who'd succeeded in the fedayeen were often the most violent—a tendency that became obvious during the war. I saw a horrific video shot by the fedayeen during battles south of Baghdad. The fedayeen had come into possession of the body of an American soldier in Samawa, in southern Iraq. They called in one of their own cameramen—the fedayeen and some Iraqi army units had their own embedded reporters who fought along with them and tried (most often failing) to send back their pictures and video from the front lines—to videotape them as they sawed off the soldier's head with a commando knife. The video was nauseating. An Iraqi reporter/fedayee (a single member of the fedayeen) embedded in this unit said the fedayeen treated the severed head like a trophy, putting it where everyone could see it during mealtimes.

After the war, the fedayeen became desperate, hunted by both the American military and most Iraqis, who hated them. Their relative weakness made it easy for Islamic extremists to hijack their fight against the Americans.

The union of the vicious fedayeen/Saddam loyalists and Sunni Muslim extremists was a symbiotic alliance. The Muslim extremists, who across the world tend to be well-organized, highly motivated and strong believers in hierarchy, gave the fedayeen a new raison d'être that was a combination of zealous Islamic dogma and Iraqi nationalism. It was Iraq's version of that age-old battle cry, "For God and Country!" But the philosophy, customized for the Iraqi experience, was more akin to "For God and Country, and the Muslim Community against Jews and Americans and Their Plots to Keep Muslims Down!" It fit right into the message Saddam Hussein had been preaching to Iraqis for decades.

The fedayeen, on the other hand, provided the Islamists with hands-on military experience and the ability to raise money by trading weapons, in addition to extorting money from local businesses, in particular jewelry shops in Baghdad owned by Iraq's Christian minority. The fedayeen also had key contacts with senior members of the former Saddam regime, who supplied them with arms, money and expertise. Specifically, the fedayeen were able to draw support from senior members of the former Iraqi armed forces, which the US administration in Iraq dissolved, creating many powerful enemies. I believe it would have been better to have kept the army intact and given it a new mission, retraining the officers and soldiers, deprogramming them of their Baathist mentality and giving the men (who after all had just fought a tough war to defend their nation against foreign aggressors) a new purpose and a belief that they were still working for the benefit of Iraq. Giving the army a national project—having the men build a new rail line or dredge the Tigris River for example—would have, in my opinion, been more useful than simply dispersing the embittered, battle-hardened fighters into a society that didn't have jobs for them or appreciate the years of sacrifices and hard living they'd endured. Instead, the US administration said that junior officers (anyone under the rank of lieutenant colonel) could join the new Iraqi army, a tiny force that couldn't accommodate most of the 400,000-strong old Iraqi army.

In the Falluja area, idle and slighted senior Iraqi military officers, fedayeen, criminals (Falluja has a history of banditry and smuggling of weapons and livestock) and Sunni extremists all came together, aided and protected by local tribes that are traditionally unfriendly to outsiders, extremely proud, vindictive and willing to fight to the death if they feel they've been disrespected. Even though most people in Falluja do not want Saddam to return to power, the Iraqi dictator has become the symbol around which the fragmented resistance groups have rallied. US forces in the area around Falluja have been bogged down in guerilla battles since April; the more they fight, the worse the situation seems to become.

* * *

Falluja—a dusty city of unfinished sand-colored two-story buildings covered with graffiti that reads AMERICA IS THE ENEMY OF GOD! and LONG LIVE SADDAM! and butcher shops displaying skinned sheep dangling upside down on meat hooks—was already dark on September 12 when the car chase that turned deadly began. The Iraqi police, reluctantly cooperating with the American forces based outside the city, were after a BMW driven by bandits wanted for holding up Iraqi and Jordanian businessmen in addition to foreign journalists. They tore along the desert road between Amman and Baghdad.

The men in the BMW opened fire on the Americans as they approached their base, evidently hoping to create a diversion. US troops—members of the no-nonsense Eighty-second Airborne Division who'd just taken over the area—unleashed a massive response, killing everyone in the BMW, eight Iraqi policemen and a Jordanian guard posted at a nearby hospital. The soldiers had responded quickly for good reason; they'd been attacked every day in and around Falluja for months.

The most common tactic has been to bury a homemade bomb—often mortars or land mines strung together with wire—and detonate it, often using a remote car door opener, as a US convoy passes. The soft-sided Humvees that most US troops travel in (which provide less protection than the lightly armored jeeps most major news agencies provide for their reporters) can do nothing to stop the blasts, let alone rocket-propelled grenades.

Although the Humvee is a convenient and fast jeep, I've never understood why US forces (especially those in such dangerous areas as Falluja) travel in such vulnerable vehicles. They don't seem to have an alternative except for the massive Bradley or other tracked armored personnel carriers—blunt tools for a peacekeeping mission. There doesn't seem to be any in-between vehicle in Iraq that is at once protected, small, maneuverable and armed with a weapon that can be used for something less than battle.

On September 7, President Bush declared that Iraq had replaced Afghanistan as the central front in the war against terrorism. Although I firmly believe the war in Iraq helped make that happen, he was nonetheless technically correct. Iraq had become a magnet for foreigners wanting to kill Americans, including members and supporters of al-Qaeda.

It became clear that the days of fedayeen and allied Islamic radicals ambushing US military convoys and tossing grenades at porn-loving soldiers were over when a car bomb exploded in front of the perimeter wall of the Jordanian embassy in Baghdad on August 7. In a single attack, the Iraqi fighters had shifted from being nationalists (for few could fault them for waging war against American troops on Iraqi soil) to terrorists, deliberately attacking unarmed civilians with the aim of causing chaos, political instability and adverse public opinion. Foreign terrorists now seemed to be involved.

A reliable fixer in Falluja (himself a former fedayee) told me he knew a group of foreign fighters in the area, and I asked him to try to set up an interview. After three weeks shuttling back and fourth between Falluja and Baghdad, he told me the group had agreed to an interview, but completely refused to allow me to go along, assuming that I worked for the CIA. I reluctantly gave him a DV camera and asked him to do the interview for me. I was suspicious about the group's credibility, worried that any Iraqi could wrap a scarf about his head, grab an RPG and claim to be a foreign fighter and issue bombastic threats. I didn't want to give airtime to an incendiary fraud. But if I could gather evidence that foreign fighters really were operating in Iraq, as analysts and US officials had repeatedly said, it would be worth it.

I sent the fixer off with a list of specific questions I hoped would help determine if the group was bluffing. I wanted to know where they'd come from, how they'd entered Iraq and when. What was the road like on the other side of the border? Who had they seen at the border, Iraqi guards or American soldiers? I wanted specific details about attacks they'd carried out. Most Iraqis, especially young people like those who inevitably appear on threatening videotapes, have never traveled outside of Iraq and would be hard-pressed to give an accurate description of Iraq's borders as seen from outside the country. It would also be obvious from their accents if they were non-Iraqis. I refused to pay any money, which may sound like the obvious ethical thing to do, but it had become standard practice among the Arab TV networks in Baghdad. The groups had come to expect it. I told the fixer to tell the men in Falluja that if they were true Islamic warriors, they wouldn't be working for money, but to defend Islam. He seemed very nervous about taking such a hard line with them. "If they're as tough as they claim, they'll be able to take it," I told him, although it did little to reassure him.

I was worried when I didn't see my fixer for the next week. I had no way of calling him and certainly wasn't going to head off to Falluja and start asking around for him, especially as he was in the midst of setting up an interview with such paranoid and violent people. The fixer finally did show up in Baghdad, apologizing for the delay. He said the group had kept postponing the appointment. First they'd agreed to meet at a farmhouse, but when he turned up, no one was there. The next day, a member of the group met the fixer at his house and escorted him to a garage. He left him inside alone and said he'd be back in ten minutes, but never returned. I think they were testing him, carrying out surveillance, watching how he reacted. A few days later, the fixer was again met at his house by several men. They told him he couldn't bring the DV camera I'd lent him. They'd brought their own old VHS camera, fearing mine contained a tracking device.

The man who spoke on the tape had a clear Syrian accent. The fixer said he'd also met Egyptians and Afghans in the course of setting up the interview. The man who appeared to be the leader of the cell—there were five masked men armed with AK-47s on the video—spoke for almost an hour. He said the men were not members of al-Qaeda, but were honored to be following the same path as Osama bin Laden. The man with the Syrian accent discussed bin Laden at length, unlike many Iraqi militant cells, which have gone out of their way to argue that their fight is a legitimate, limited struggle to shake off American occupation. The Syrian also called on Iraqis to work together to liberate Baghdad, once capital of the Islamic world. He said "thousands" of fighters like him had crossed into Iraq and that the country's open borders had made it easy. He was right about the open borders.

It didn't take long to find a smuggler who agreed to take me across the border into Iran. He was very relaxed when we met at his home in Baghdad and plotted our mission over bottles of orange soda. "You want to go to Iran? Sure, anytime," said the heavyset man, a Kurd from a small town near the Iranian border about 150 miles northeast of Baghdad. The smuggler had relatives in Iran who helped him ferry people back and forth across the border several times a week. He boasted he could take me to Tehran if I wanted. I told him that I only wanted to cross five feet into Iran and then come back. I wanted to find out how difficult it was, not emigrate.

Two days later, the smuggler and I set off at five in the morning in his right-hand-drive Toyota, an anomaly, since cars in Iraq have their steering wheels on the left side. He'd bought it very cheap because nobody had wanted it. It was still dark as we shared a breakfast of cans of orange soda (his favorite, I discovered), local cigarettes and an Iraqi version of Turkish delight flavored with rosewater. It made me somewhat sick. We were listening to Feirooz's sweet, undulating voice on the radio as we drove north, passing little industrial villages bustling with metal shops, garages and brick factories. There was a heavy US military presence on the road, and we had driven through four checkpoints by the time we reached Khanaqin, a Kurdish city near the Iranian border suffering obvious neglect. But despite the crumbling buildings and roads filled with potholes, the mood in Khanaqin was remarkably pleasant. There was no tension, and US troops at a base in the city weren't wearing their flak jackets. The markets were bustling with customers, and Kurdish militiamen patrolled the streets in jeeps that looked like they'd been around since World War II; they'd actually been looted from Iraqi army bases.

The smuggler and I pushed farther north, taking a small paved road that ran along the Iranian border. It was exhilarating to be in this area, which under Saddam had been completely off-limits. We passed tiny mud villages populated by single families of goat and sheep herders. Some of the families had only recently moved back into their homes. Saddam had pushed Kurds away from the border area, fearing they'd be disloyal during his disastrous war with Iran. In an act of pure ethnic cleansing, Saddam had transplanted entire Kurdish villages, moving in Sunni families he thought he could trust. Now the

Kurds were coming back, pushing out the Sunnis, including some people who'd been in the area originally. I could see Iranian guard towers less than a kilometer from the road. Some of them seemed to be abandoned. I asked the smuggler what stopped him from driving off the road and into Iran. "Nothing," he said. "But there are a few minefields. Do you want to do it?" I declined, and we pushed farther north to a village pressed up against the Iranian border, and where my driver said there were dirt paths that would take me into Iran. About an hour later we arrived at one of the dirt roads the smuggler was talking about. We turned onto it, but as we rounded a bend we were both surprised to see a Kurdish checkpoint. "Don't worry," the smuggler said, confident he could talk us through. But the Kurds were very thorough and didn't like the fact that I had a DV camera and a Thuraya telephone. The smuggler, speaking to them in Kurdish, said we were tourists. They didn't believe him for a second and took us into custody.

The guards escorted us to a Kurdish base a few hundred yards from the checkpoint. In the car, I asked the smuggler—somewhat annoyed—why he hadn't anticipated this problem, implying with the tone of my voice, *What kind of lousy smuggler are you?*

I spoke to the Kurdish base commander before the smuggler started making up stories. I told him I was a journalist working on a story about Iraq's porous borders. The commander—wearing the pea green uniform and baggy pants of a *peshmerga* fighter—turned out to be exceptionally cooperative. He was very pro-American, respected the commander of the Fourth Infantry Division in the area, and gave me a lengthy tour of the base. He even dispatched one of his three pickup trucks to take me to see the dirt paths smugglers were using to cross in from Iran. We had to walk the last kilometer of the rocky hilly road, which was covered with fresh donkey droppings, evidence it had recently been used.

The base commander said smugglers had been using the dirt paths for years, mostly sending alcohol into the Islamic Republic of Iran in exchange for drugs and weapons. The base commander understood Arabic but preferred to speak in Kurdish, which I don't understand, so my smuggler, ironically, became my translator.

The base commander told me human trafficking had become a major problem after the war and that he caught dozens of Iranians and Afghans every week. He'd arrested forty Afghans two weeks earlier and seven the day before I arrived. He showed me the truck they'd been driving in, dented on one side after the Afghans flipped over during a chase, killing one man, who the Kurds then buried amid high reeds a few hundred yards from the base camp. I couldn't contain my laughter as my smuggler translated the commander's complaints about "specialists" who brought people in and out of Iran. The base commander also introduced me to three Iranian detainees he had under guard. They were sitting on a blanket on the ground in the shade of a cement holding cell where they slept. The base commander said he was waiting to arrest more and that once he'd taken ten into custody he'd have a pickup truck take them all to Sulaimaniya, where he'd hand them over to the Americans. The Iranians—believing I was somehow interrogating them—pleadingly told me they'd come into Iraq to visit Karbala and Najaf, the two holy Shiite cities south of Baghdad. The commander told me he tended to believe them. That's why most of the Iranians came into Iraq, he said. Before the war, Saddam Hussein permitted only a limited number of Iranians—nearly all of them Shiite Muslims—to make pilgrimages to Najaf and Karbala. Now they all wanted to do it.

It was the Afghans the Kurdish base commander didn't like. He suspected some of them were members of Ansar al-Islam, a militant group linked to al-Qaeda, which had bases in Kurdish parts of northern Iraq destroyed by US forces during the war. The border commander said some of the Ansar al-Islam fighters had fled into the mountainous border zone to escape the heavy fighting and were crossing back into Iraq to resume their activities.

Foreign fighters were coming not only across the hilly border from Iran, but also from Syria and, to a lesser degree, Saudi Arabia, according to US officials.

Like US authorities in Iraq, I suspect foreign fighters—Islamic fanatics of the same type attracted to the wars in which Muslims are involved around the world and represented by al-Qaeda (their bloodthirsty veterans union)—were involved at some level in the bombing of the Jordanian embassy. The attack represented a shift that was too great for there not to have been some type of outside influence. The Jordanian embassy was also a target that both foreign militant groups and the fedayeen/Saddam loyalists could agree on. The foreign militants liked it because it expanded the scope of what had thus far been a very local guerilla war in Iraq. Attacking a foreign embassy transformed the fight into a global struggle and a global jihad. For the Baath party and fedayeen, the attack was revenge against Jordan for having cooperated with the Americans during the war. Jordan had supported Saddam during the 1991 Gulf War, a favor Saddam had repaid by supplying Jordan with fuel for pennies a gallon. But Jordan failed to come to Saddam's side in Gulf War II. Saddam's allies felt they'd been double-crossed. The marriage of local and international interests was repeated in the bombing of the UN headquarters in Baghdad two weeks later.

The car bomb that exploded in front of the United Nations headquarters in Baghdad was a clear indication that the militant groups operating in Iraq now believed themselves to be players in world politics capable of influencing US foreign policy. I believe the bombing, in which twenty-two people were killed, including Sergio Vieira de Mello, UN Secretary-General Kofi Annan's respected and popular envoy, was specifically an attempt to isolate the United States internationally and keep the UN from playing a greater role in Iraq.

In the days preceding the UN bombing, the Bush administration had been floating the idea that it wanted to increase the UN's involvement in post-war Iraq—an important, necessary step that would give the US occupation and state-building efforts much-needed international legitimacy and, it was hoped, support in terms of peacekeepers and money. Militant groups fighting in Iraq simply don't want the Americans to have this backing, because it undercuts their claim to be fighting a legitimate war against occupation.

The attack against the UN headquarters, and another failed suicide bombing less than five weeks later in the parking lot, had the added effect of crippling the UN's humanitarian programs in Iraq—a bonus for militant groups because the less progress the Iraqi people see on the ground, the less they support American/international efforts in Iraq. It's the same reason saboteurs have been blowing up oil pipelines.

But it was the car bombing against the Shiite Ayatollah Mohammed Bakr al-Hakim in Najaf on August 29 that had the most profound impact on Iraqi society and that revealed the depth of the problems and challenges Iraq will face in the coming years.

Al-Hakim had just finished leading the Friday prayers at the Imam Ali Shrine when the bomb went off. The explosive was so powerful that it killed more than a hundred of al-Hakim's supporters and stripped some of the survivors naked, literally blowing off their clothing. Only al-Hakim's hand, pen, wedding band and watch were found. Shrapnel from the bomb also damaged the blue and green tiled façade of the Imam Ali Shrine, one of the most holy sites for the world's 120 million Shiite Muslims.

Shia Islam began in the seventh century over a succession battle following the death of the Muslim Prophet Mohammed in A.D. 632. Sunni or "orthodox" Muslims accepted Mohammed's respected confidant Abu Bakr as the new caliph, or leader, of the rapidly expanding Muslim empire. A smaller group, however, believed that the much younger Ali bin Abi Talib, Mohammed's cousin and son-in-law, deserved the position. His followers became known as the *shi'at Ali*, or "party of Ali," later known simply as the Shiites.

Ali did eventually become Islam's fourth caliph in A.D. 656, but the schism over succession was never settled and occasionally erupted into bloody disputes. After ruling for five years, Ali was murdered in a feud, as was his son (Mohammed's grandson) Hussein. Ali was buried in Najaf and Hussein was put to rest twenty miles north in Karbala.

Many Shiite Muslims today hope to be buried like Ali in Najaf, and after the war, Iranians started paying Iraqi middlemen to bury their dead relatives in the holy city's massive cemetery. Some disreputable middlemen, however, have been known to simply dump the corpses by the side of the road.

Al-Hakim had returned to Iraq only four months before he was killed, after having spent more than two decades in exile in Iran, where he'd led the al-Badr Brigades, a well-armed, Iranian-trained guerilla army that fought against Saddam Hussein. After his return, al-Hakim quickly established himself as one of the three main Shiite merja presiding over Iraq's *hawza*, a network of Shiite seminaries and religious schools based in Najaf. The power and influence of the hawza should not be underestimated. It is the body that will determine how most of Iraq looks and feels in the coming years.

The hawza is not housed in a single building, nor does it have a single leader. Instead, it is a dynamic network of Shiite schools, courts, holy sites and Shiite prayer centers, called *husseiyaat*, named after Ali's martyred son Hussein. For the past three decades, Saddam Hussein and his secular Baath party crushed the power and influence of Iraq's hawza. Saddam also limited the number of husseiyaat that could be opened, and assassinated Iraq's leading Shiite figures, including, in 1999, the immensely popular merja, the Grand Ayatollah Mohammed Sadiq al-Sadr. After Saddam was toppled, Shiite Muslims in Baghdad renamed the slum of Saddam City "Sadr City" to honor the late grand ayatollah.

After returning from Iran, al-Hakim embarked on his mission to both revitalize Iraq's hawza and, whenever possible, make sure he led as much of it as possible. It was the exact same goal pursued by the other Shiite merja in Iraq, the late grand ayatollah's son Muqtada al-Sadr and the Grand Ayatollah Ali al-Sistani. Their simultaneous efforts produced internal rivalries among Shiites, but more important, dramatically increased the influence of the hawza in Iraq. Every day since the end of the war, new husseiyaat have been opened across Iraq, especially in Baghdad, some of them on land Shiites don't own. The Shiites have also been unilaterally renaming streets throughout the Iraqi capital after famous clerics and opening hawza schools throughout Iraq. Six months after Saddam was toppled and the Baath party removed, the Shiite hawza has transformed itself from a beaten-down network of clerics into the most powerful and influential body in Iraq. The hawza—through the merja who lead it—has been able to organize religious festivals, bringing together millions of Shiites, and after al-Hakim's death, organize their own security. Iraqi police don't go near Shiite religious processions. They merely cordon off the area and leave the rest to the hawza.

The American administration in Iraq is undoubtedly aware of the rise of Shiite power in the country, but has largely been unwilling, or potentially unable, to challenge it. Nor have the Americans felt the immediate need to do so, because the Shiite merja have been tolerant of the Americans. The general Shiite strategy in Iraq has been to allow the Americans to stabilize the country, spend tens of billions of dollars on reconstruction, and kill off the remaining Baath party/Sunni extremists, while they focus on making Iraq's hawza more powerful than the rival hawza that has gained strength up in Iran over the last several decades to fill the power vacuum in the Shiite world created by Saddam's oppression of Shiites in Iraq. Quite simply, they have chosen to be patient, allow the Americans to complete their mission in Iraq, and then take over. It's a vision that frightens Iraq's Sunni Muslim population and makes those living in places like Falluja and Baghdad feel squeezed and threatened. It's pushing them to fight. The killing of al-Hakim was an attempt to stop this trend, both by the Saddam loyalists and fedayeen (who like many Iraqis don't want an Islamic state in Iraq, especially one run by Shiites) and al-Qaeda and al-Qaeda–type militants who consider Shiite Muslims to be rebels who've divided the Muslim world for thirteen hundred years. Sunni Muslims also criticize Shiites for giving Ali and Hussein a saint-like status, in contradiction to the tenets of Islam.

But far from stopping the Shiites' march to power, the assassination of al-Hakim only convinced Shiites to redouble their efforts to rebuild the hawza and solidify their power base. The attack also injected a troubling air of militancy into the Shiite revival movement in Iraq and led to the proliferation of Shiite militia groups.

After al-Hakim's death, the al-Badr Brigades—which traveled with al-Hakim to Iran—took to the streets of Najaf, armed with assault rifles. They set up checkpoints and threatened foreign journalists. Their anger was directed both against Baath party members and al-Qaeda supporters, whom they blamed for jointly carrying out the attack, and also against the Americans, whom they accused of not doing enough to protect the holy city. The al-Badr Brigades and local Shiite tribes launched an independent investigation and seized at least two and as many as six men they said belonged to al-Qaeda. After attempting to demand a bounty for them, the tribes eventually handed at least two suspects over to American authorities, according to a member of one of the tribes involved.

It is highly significant that the Americans did nothing to

stop the Shiite militias or disarm them. Instead, in an acknowledgment of their influence, the Bremer administration chose to regulate them, requiring the militias to coordinate their activities with local Iraqi police. The Americans clearly didn't want to be in a position in which US troops were trying to take guns out of the Shiites' hands, especially after al-Hakim's murder. It could have started a war with the Shiites, the last thing the Americans need.

By legitimizing the militias, the Americans also were able to influence which Shiite militia groups operate in the country. The Americans tolerated the al-Badr Brigades mainly because al-Hakim had supported the US-appointed Iraqi governing council; al-Hakim's brother was one of the founding members. The regulated al-Badr Brigades also acted to counterbalance the militant followers of the firebrand Moqtada al-Sadr.

Since the fall of Saddam, Muqtada al-Sadr has tried to make himself into the leader of Iraq's hawza. His strategy has been to tap into the general public's deep-seated mistrust of the Americans, a sentiment prevalent across the Middle East and especially in Iraq, where anti-American dogma was the backbone of the state's foreign policy and propaganda for decades. Muqtada al-Sadr has declared that only the hawza can protect Shiite rights, religious leaders and holy places. He has begun to set up an all-Shiite army—the jeish al-Mahdi—to carry out this mission. The young al-Sadr has already collected tens of thousands of signatures for volunteers for his jeish al-Mahdi, diligently registering all of them at Najaf's local courthouse—proof of his growing power base for all to see. Al-Sadr's spokespeople say the jeish al-Mahdi will eventually be armed. Al-Sadr hopes the jeish al-Mahdi will become the army of the hawza and that he will be its commander in chief, a position that would certainly propel him to the top of the Shiite pantheon, a goal that became somewhat more obtainable after al-Hakim's murder. Some Iraqis in fact have suggested that Muqtada al-Sadr may have been involved in al-Hakim's assassination, although there's been no evidence to support the accusation. Al-Sadr's proactive approach stands in stark contrast to the behavior of Iraq's single most powerful and respected Shiite merja, the seventy-three-year-old Grand Ayatollah Ali al-Sistani.

Al-Sistani has not openly embraced the political process, rarely giving interviews or commenting on earthly matters. His life is the hawza. He does have a broad political objective, but it is much more subtle than the rabble-rousing al-Sadr's. Al-Sistani also seeks for the hawza to rule Iraq and has called for immediate elections in the country, in contrast to the US plan to first draw up a constitution. The US proposal is that it will supervise the writing of the constitution and that elections will then be held based on the principles put forward in that—US-approved—document. Al-Sistani's approach would guarantee a much greater role for the hawza, because Shiites, as Iraq's disciplined, more-or-less unified majority (Shiites in Iraq are divided over which merja they support, but most agree on the sanctity of the hawza), would clearly emerge on top and would then be in a strong position to write a constitution without the Americans involved in the drafting process and thereby limiting the extent to which Iraq could become a democracy.

AFTERWORD

DURING THE FIRST SIX MONTHS after the war in Iraq, the country separated itself roughly along ethnic lines into three distinct regions: the Kurdish north, the Sunni triangle and the Shiite south. Today, the regions already operate as if they were three separate countries. These divisions, which predated the war but were suppressed by Saddam's blanket rule of fear, are likely to increase over the years and will have profound implications as Iraq and the Middle East try to rebuild after the war.

The Kurdish north has become a pro-American haven where people continue to be thankful that the United States rid them of Saddam. After all, in 1987 and 1988 Saddam used chemical weapons (a mixture of mustard gas and nerve agents) against forty Kurdish villages, the worst of which was in the town of Halabja, killing five thousand and injuring ten thousand. The US forces and the Kurds have been cooperating well, and as long as the Americans have influence in Iraq it seems that they will reward the Kurds whenever they have a chance.

But there are potential threats in the Kurdish areas too. The Kurds have long wanted to establish an independent state of Kurdistan, a nationalistic desire that neighboring Turkey in particular opposes because of its own large Kurdish population. If Iraq fails as a state or becomes too religiously extreme, the Kurds will likely revitalize these national aspirations. The Kurds have also been plagued for years by infighting, which could reemerge once the euphoria of Saddam's removal wears off.

While the potential problems in the Kurdish areas seem to be somewhat far off, the Sunni triangle in central and western Iraq is likely to be a bleeding wound for the Americans until they pull out of Iraq. The Sunnis have not only lost their privileged status under Saddam, but they also feel squeezed by the Kurds in the north and, more acutely, by the Shiites in the south and in Baghdad. The Sunnis, who've ruled Iraq since the state was founded after World War I, feel they have the right to be in charge, a position that neighboring Sunni Muslim states Syria, Saudi Arabia and Jordan may tend to agree with, especially if Iraqi Shiites start to cause problems for them.

Also troubling is the new radical Islamic dimension to the militant movement against US forces in the Sunni triangle. This movement has become a jihad aided by foreign zealots who are either members of al-Qaeda or supporters of the group. These radicals have no interest in reaching any type of compromise with the Americans and can only be defeated by being rooted out. If they succeed in killing many Americans in Iraq, however, it could be the new impetus that al-Qaeda needs to attract supporters and finances to counteract the damage done by the US-led war on terrorism. Moreover, Iraq has become a training ground par excellence, where militants have been getting real fighting skills and learning to counter American military tactics; it is much better than the training the militants were getting by diving through a few flaming hoops at al-Qaeda bases in Afghanistan.

The only way to achieve success in cities in the Sunni triangle seems to be by winning the trust of the local tribes, not by frightening or trying to defeat them. Attacking them only triggers their pride, at which point they stop thinking. If, however, the tribal leaders see benefits—schools, hospitals and power—and can be convinced that their local influence is being respected and maintained, they might be willing to cooperate with the Americans. It's not going to be easy, because every time the Americans kill an Iraqi—inevitable as US troops launch counterattacks or fight the people who plant roadside bombs every day—it becomes harder to tell the tribal leaders that it's the Americans who are, as the troops in Iraq like to say, "the good guys" and that they should sell out their fellow Sunnis.

But it's the Shiite south and Baghdad that are likely to determine what Iraq eventually looks and feels like in the coming decade. While there are undoubtedly many secular Shiites who fear an Islamic state, it's the merja who have been setting the political agenda in post-war Iraq. Their strategy has been to focus internally and stay out of the Americans' way.

There are many possible problems that could arise from the unchecked rise of the Shiite clergy. Iraq was a secular dictatorship for decades and, while no one liked it, Iraqis—especially the Kurds and Baghdad's educated elite—will not accept too many Islamic restrictions imposed on their lives.

But it will not be easy for the Americans to limit the Shiites' political ambitions. Since the war, the Shiites have been somewhat drunk on their newfound power and will not respond well if the Americans try to clip their wings. The Shiites are quiet now, but if after a year or so they don't feel that they've been given the autonomy and authority they expect—powers they feel they deserve after years of repression—that could easily change. Already, every time Shiite leaders feel threatened (in particular Muqtada al-Sadr), they have organized protest rallies involving tens of thousands of people. They've been saber-rattling exercises, which have frightened both the American administration in Iraq and just about everyone else in the country.

Despite the many challenges Iraq faces, however, I am generally optimistic when I look back at what Iraq was before, during and after the war, mainly because it was so horrendous before. Under Saddam, Iraq was a state in which everyone was constantly afraid. I believe the war to remove Saddam and his horrific system of government was brave, and if in fact it was the main motivation for the war it was just and noble. The problem, however, was that the Bush administration only pre-

sented the human rights argument to the American people as
the third and weakest motivation for war, trailing Iraq's alleged
weapons of mass destruction program and the regime's links to
international terrorists.

Furthermore, I don't think that there was any reason for
the United States to have led the incursion with so little international support or to have been in such a rush to attack Iraq.
If the world changed after the attacks of September 11, 2001,
it wasn't because of Saddam. Saddam was a monster to his
own people, but was not a supporter of Islamic fundamentalists like Osama bin Laden. He killed people like bin Laden.

Saddam did, however, seem to have been interested in
developing weapons of mass destruction, and if such a discov-
ery is made it would add a clear motivation. Saddam Hussein
should never have been allowed to have chemical, biological
or nuclear weapons. The power would have gone to his head.

While the American military didn't need any help to defeat
Iraq, the biggest problem the United States faces by having led
the war is mainly a psychological one. The Americans have
simply taken on too much responsibility in Iraq. If the lights go
out in Baghdad in 2010, or a future Iraqi politician steals from
his own people, there will be many Iraqis who will point the
finger of blame at the Americans, arguing that they're responsible because they set up the system. The same goes for the Iraqi
constitution. No matter how sound the founding document is,
Iraqis will have to continuously defend themselves against accusations—both at home and throughout the Arab world—that
they are governed by an American creation. This could even

tempt some Iraqis to go out of their way to be anti-American as a way to prove their independence. And the capture of Saddam will have a greater impact in Washington than in Baghdad. While his arrest has dispirited some of his hardcore loyalists, by December 13 the majority of the militants had adopted a new Islamist/anti-occupation ideology. Saddam had become little more than a symbol to them, which he will likely remain.

I am nonetheless optimistic about Iraq's future. Since the 1991 Gulf War, Iraq had gone backward, slipping into economic destitution and committing some of the worst human rights abuses imaginable. I am confident that in ten years Iraqis will be better off than they are today, although the ride will certainly be bumpy. The Americans are spending vast amounts of money to rebuild schools and power plants, and to institute sewers and a mobile phone network, the latter banned by Saddam for security reasons. Soon the country will be part of the international community, trading the oil it hasn't been able to capitalize on for a decade.

Making Iraq succeed is also essential for American foreign policy in the Middle East. Washington's long-term credibility in the region is on the line. If the Americans can help turn Iraq into a democracy that is a model for the rest of the Arab world, it would be a truly historic accomplishment. If the state fails, the Americans will be mistrusted in the region for another generation.

A free, freethinking Iraq could also serve to calm Israel, since Israel would no longer have an aggressive state in missile range to the west, and a calm Israel could help to restart the

Israeli-Palestinian peace process. Now is the time for Americans to be actively engaged in the region and to use Iraq's reconstruction as an opportunity to build friends and trust, but it's an extremely delicate time because there hasn't been such a radical rewriting of the Middle East map since World War I. What will emerge from this chaos is uncertain, but there is the opportunity for the new Iraq to usher in hope for an entirely new Middle East. The alternative is an unstable Iraq that encourages fanaticism and terrorism and will mire the region in turmoil for decades to come. Iraq can be an example of an American success in the Middle East or of an American failure that detractors will be quick to capitalize on.

INDEX